T0149749

A COMMENTARY
THE BOOK OF GENESIS

DR. JOHN THOMAS WYLIE

authorHOUSE

AuthorHouse™
1663 Liberty Drive
Bloomington, IN 47403
www.authorhouse.com
Phone: 1 (800) 839-8640

Published by AuthorHouse 06/12/2018

ISBN: 978-1-5462-4638-1 (sc)
ISBN: 978-1-5462-4637-4 (e)

Print information available on the last page.

CONTENTS

INTRODUCTION

Genesis

Beginning, the first book of the Old Testament. It is called "Beginning," since it gives a record of the "Eras" of man (Gen. 2:4). It might be isolated into two sections: the historical backdrop of four patriarchs. The writer was Moses, and the book uncovers the birthplace of the world, follows the start of the Hebrew country in Abraham, follows the historical backdrop of the picked individuals through the eras of Abraham, Issac, Jacob, and the children of Jacob, particularly Joseph, until the passageway into Egypt. The book closes with the demise of Joseph, yet ought to be perused consistently through to the following book moreover.

The Title

The word Genesis came into English by method for Latin from the Greek. In the Septuagint (LXX), it framed the superscription for the main book of the Bible. The word signifies "inception, source, or siring." The Hebrew word b'r'eshith, interpreted "in (the) start," is the principal word in the Hebrew Bible. It is much of the time used to assign the book of Genesis.

Nature

Beginning is the book of causes (origins). It gives a glorious record of the beginnings of all the Creator brought into being. It answers men's inquiries concerning the birthplace of the world, and of plant, creature, and human life. It recounts the foundation of the family, the source of wrongdoing, the giving of the awesome disclosure, the development and advancement of the race, and the introduction of God's intend to realize reclamation through his picked individuals. It displays and shows interminable facts, and it settle conundrums, secrets, and perplexing circumstances in the light of God's will for his kin. In clear, important dialect the essayist puts forward God's uncovered plans and purposes, and the wonders of his dealings with men.

Beginning takes the peruser back to the terrifically essential snapshot of creation when the supreme Creator talked into being the inimitable marvels of sun, moon, stars, planets, worlds, plants, and moving animals, and the one whom he made in his picture.

In these fifty sections the enlivened essayist unfurls the dramatization of creation; he tells how sin came stealthily and tirelessly to bring ruin, distortion, and passing; he uncovers the unfortunate products of wrongdoing in our first guardians' despicable thrashing; and he indicates how later, the amassed evil of men conveyed decimation and nearly demolition to human culture.

In the crisp starting the author follows the development of the new race, lastly the energizing professions of Abraham, Isaac, Jacob, and Jacob's kids. The book closes with the passing of Joseph in the place that is known as the land of Egypt.

Beginning 1-11 exhibits the record of man from creation to the start of the life of Abraham. Beginning 12-50 describes God's dealings with his picked human Abraham, Isaac, Jacob, Joseph, and their relatives. All through the story, the creator's main concern is to set forward Jehovah's motivation in making and fortunately controlling such a choose people. Genesis, as well as the entire Bible demonstrates that through the organization of this individuals, the Lord looked to uncover his temperament and approaches to the world, to build up his heavenly will in the earth, and to bring "uplifting news" of recovery to all men. Countries and people are said and depicted in the book just as they fit into the Lord's magnificent arrangement and reason. Sumerians, Hittites, Babylonians, and Assyrians, at whatever point their history influences that of the picked individuals, enter the photo quickly so as to show God's motivation for the world. At each progression, the Spirit looked to influence the disclosure to clear to men of any age. In the quickly moving dramatization, the arrangement of God was unfolding.

Authorship

It is protected to assert Moses as the capable writer of the book. It is the main book of the Pentateuch, which both Scripture and convention credit to Moses. It is hard to discover a man in all the scope of Israel's life who was better fit the bill to compose this history. Prepared in the "intelligence of the Egyptians" (Acts 7:22), Moses was fortunately arranged to comprehend accessible records, original copies, and oral stories. As a prophet to whom was conceded the bizarre benefit of unhurried hours of fellowship with God on Sinai, he was very much prepared to record for all eras the Lord's depiction of his movement through the ages. What other individual in every one of the hundreds of years had such powers and such confidence, and delighted in such personal association with Jehovah?

The revelation in present day times of such old records as the Amarna Letters, the Ugaritic (or Ras Shamra) writing, and the dirt tablets from Mesopotamia to recreate the chronicled and social foundation of the Biblical record, and to find what life resembled in Egypt, Palestine, and Mesopotamia amid the Biblical age. Likely numerous oral and composed records, reachings far once again into artifact, were accessible to the recognized Hebrew researcher, whose Egyptian tutoring and whose graduate investigation in the district of Mount Sinai made him mindful of huge world developments. As indicated by

Jewish custom, when the colossal recorder Ezra returned from Babylonia to Jerusalem, bringing the Hebrew compositions of the Old Testament, he set to work with gigantic vitality safeguarding, duplicating, and altering the old materials in his ownership.

Genesis And Science

In the event that an understudy hopes to discover a Genesis a logical record of how the world appeared, with all inquiries concerning primitive life replied in specialized dialect commonplace to the educator or understudy of science, he will be frustrated. Beginning is not an endeavor to ponder or answer such specialized inquiries. It manages matters a long ways past the domain of science. The creator tries to acquire us touch with the endless God and to uncover the consecrated significance of his being, his motivation, and his dealings with his animals as he works out his sacred significance and good commendation, it respect and loftiness, pictures the unceasing God at work setting up a place where his cherished animals can live and develop and uncover the celestial greatness.

CHAPTER

ONE

The Early Beginnings
(1:1-11:32)

The Creation
(1:1-2:25)

God is the Creator of all things. From the start in the Book of Genesis, the concentration of the solid light of disclosure turns upon the Almighty. He is the Beginning, the Cause, the Source of all that is. He brought into being every one of the things and the people that were to fit into his arrangement for the ages. All the issue vital for his later working, he supernaturally made.

1. In beginning (b'r'eshith). The writer takes the peruser back before time, into the unimaginable ranges of endlessness, however dialect comes up short him as he tries to propose the condition of things before time was. He gives no trace of a substantial date for this "starting." His record comes to once more into the time before the dating of occasions. "God made." The magnificent conviction of disclosure depends on this one strong affirmation. God did it. Nothing additionally bewildering could

be proclaimed. 'ELohim is the standard word for "God" in Hebrew, Aramaic, and Arabic. It is really plural in frame, however it is utilized with a verb in the particular. Maybe the plural is best clarified as specifying "abundance of might" or excellent respect and boundless enormity. In this One are joined every one of the forces of time everlasting and boundlessness.

"Created" (baara') is a verb utilized only of God. Man couldn't reach up to the forces characteristic in this word, for it depicts full marvel. By the sovereign, originative energy of God something completely new was brought into being.

"The heavens and the earth." Here the creator centers enthusiasm upon every one of the territories of the world above, around, and underneath. In this expression he incorporates the finished universe as it was known (or may come to be known) by the Hebrews, and all the crude material expected to make suns, planets, stars, nebulae, cosmic systems, particles, molecules, electrons, and all the particular things and creatures on the earth.

Men of science uncover that our universe contains more than 100 billion stars, and that our sun is 150 trillion miles from the focal point of our world. Our cosmic system is one of a little group of 19 worlds, the closest of which is 30 million light a very long time from us (150 million trillion miles).

Our examination researchers, by utilizing capable telescopes, have ensured that there are more than a billion universes. They assess the quantity of stars in these cosmic systems as near 100 quintillion. The flame energy of one of the universes is equivalent to that of 400 million suns. As man looks on this immense creation and contrasts what he sees and the enlivened author's record of its birthplace, his heart must be loaded with wonderment.

He perceives the hand of God in the excellence and request of the close planetary system and in the power at the focal point of the iota. Regardless of whether he looks upon the sun (decidedly charged), holding the planets (contrarily charged), or whether he inspects the core (emphatically charged) at the core of the molecule, holding every electron (adversely charged) in its influence, he detects the astuteness, power, and magnificence of God. In the light of this, a respectful man bows before his Creator in amazement and honest to goodness commitment, and spills out love, reverence, thanksgiving, and intemperate acclaim. The eminent formation of the Lord is that being, enormously cherished, whom he made in his image.

2. "The earth was without form, and void" (tohu wabohu). The inspired author rapidly turns his consideration regarding the earth, for his story needs to do with God's designs and arrangement for human life on this planet. He portrays the earth in its incomplete state. There was a lot of material within reach for each work God intended to make, however in a tumultuous state-squander, void, dim. Six full innovative days were to roll out wonderful improvements. God's motivation couldn't be fulfilled until the point when his phenomenal touch had made a big deal about this turmoil. Indeed, even murkiness (frequently, in Scripture, related with abhorrent) was to be made subservient to his will. "The Spirit of God was drifting" (ruah...m'rahepet). The words depict the vitality giving nearness of God, swathing and touching the disarray and incomplete earth as he arranged to finish his creation. Like a dedicated mother

winged creature, he moved about, pampering his adoration on the infant world.

3. "Then said God, Let there be light." The author introduces God's first imaginative word. No sweat and consider awareness, the all-powerful God brought light into reality. He articulated his statement, and immediately his will was refined (Ps. 33:6,9). Light was God's response to the strength of murkiness. It was the Lord's first positive advance toward finishing the full program of creation. Without it, alternate strides would have been pointless. The Apostle John discloses to us that "God is light" (1 John 1:5).

4. "God saw...that it was good." When the Creator looked upon the item total and outstanding; and he was satisfied. Seven times this announcement is made. Each one of God's inventive demonstrations was immaculate, finished, satisfying, fulfilling. it regards recollect this was a similar light man sees and appreciates today.

5. "Evening and morning." In the book of Genesis evening dependably goes before morning. The production of light finished the rule of obscurity and expedited the primary day.

Since it was still some time before the making of the sun and moon, it is inaccurate to talk about real twenty-four hour days until after that point in the program of the Creator. The reference here is to a day of God, and not to a normal day limited by minutes and hours. The start of each demonstration of creation is called morning, and the end of that particular heavenly act is called evening.

6. "An firmament (expanse) amidst the waters." The Hebrew word raqia speaks to something prevailed over or squeezed out in order to reach out finished a wide surface. The essayist proposes here a territory over the earth, holding immense repositories of water to be discharged for rain.

9. "Let the dry land appear." At one phase, water secured everything. On the third day, be that as it may, the Lord made the land and the vegetable kingdom. By his awesome power he made the land rise up out of the immense mass of waters, and framed the earth (cf. Ps. 104:608); Job 38:8-11). From the dirt, at the express order of God, living vegetation sprang forward, and soon dressed the earth with magnificence and gave nourishment to living animals.

14. "Let there be lights." Hebrew m'orot depicts the illuminating presences or instruments of light. By methods for these illuminating presences, the earth got the light fundamental for looking after life. They were to "control" throughout the day and the night (v.16), to be for signs and seasons, and to give light upon the earth. The record influences it to clear that God made them and after that set them set up. As indicated by the heavenly outline, the sun, moon, and stars were altogether conveyed into being to do his particular will.

20. "Let the waters swarm with swarms of living creatures." This verse depicts the sudden happening to hosts of winged things and fishes. They were intended to give another obvious exhibit of the Creator's energy. With their appearance, there was life on earth and furthermore action. What's more, there was, besides, an unending progression of living animals, all made by God's relentless hand.

21. "Sea Monsters" (AV, extraordinary whales). Truly, extended creatures that crawl, slither, or coast upon the earth, in or out of the water, for example, serpents, eels, fish, and mythical beasts.

22. The Lord inhaled his approval upon these and instructed them to be "productive and Multiply." The advance of God's imaginative action was upward toward the formation of man.

26. "Let us make man." The preeminent snapshot of creation landed as God made man. The account presents God as approaching the glorious court, or the other two individuals from the Trinity, to focus all consideration on this occasion. A few observers, be that as it may, translate the plural as a "plural of magnificence," demonstrating nobility and enormity. The plural type of the word for God, "Elohim, can be clarified in to some degree a similar way. The Lord is spoken to as giving uncommon consideration to an issue laden with much hugeness.

"In our Image" (selem), "after our resemblance" (d'mut). AThough these two equivalent words have isolate implications, there is here apparently no push to exhibit diverse parts of God's being. Unmistakably man, as God made him, was particularly unique in relation to the creatures as of now made. He remained on a considerably higher level, for God made him to be godlike, and made him His very own uncommon picture time everlasting. Man was an animal with whom his Maker could visit and have association and fellowship. Then again, the Lord could anticipate that man will answer him and be mindful to him. Man was constituted to have the benefit of decision, even to the point of defying his Creator. He was to be God's capable agent and steward on the earth, to work out his Creator's will and satisfy the perfect reason. World domain was to be conceded to this new animal (cf. Ps. 8:5-7). He was dispatched to repress (kabash, "tread upon") the earth, and to take after God's arrangement in filling it with individuals. This wonderful animal, with his fantastic benefits and overwhelming duties, was to live and move in royal form.

31. "Very Good" (tob m'od). At the point when the Lord looked upon the finished consequence of his innovative demonstrations, he communicated impossible to miss enjoyment and extraordinary fulfillment. Everything in the universe, from the greatest star to the littlest piece of turf, conveyed bliss to his heart. It was an excellent ensemble. The Creator's fulfillment is here communicated in pithy yet clear dialect.

CHAPTER

TWO

The Creation Of Man
(2:1-25)

1,2. "Finished (kalah)……... rested (shabat)……." hallowed (kadash). At the point when the Creator had articulated his endorsement of all that he had made, including man, the crown of creation, he proclaimed the work wrapped up. For the present, he would embrace no further creation. Nonetheless, he purified, or "consecrated," a day of finish rest. The Hebrew word shabat can be deciphered "halted" or "stopped" or "cut off." During this time even God would rest from inventive movement (cf. Ex. 20:11; 31:17).

3. The "seventh day" was separate to be sacrosanct and regarded during that time as an update that God had named a period of rest, refreshment, and finish end of all customary work, drudge, and battle.

4. "These are the generations" (toldot). The Hebrew word originates from a verb importance to sire or bear kids. It could be interpreted "begettings." This announcement might be a reference to Genesis 1. The LXX interprets: This is the Book of the Genesis. Some would

decipher it, The historical backdrop of the sky and the earth. The posterity of paradise and earth were along these lines imagined.

"Jehovah, the Lord God." For the first run through, the name Yahweh, or Jehovah (cf. Exod. 6:2,3) is exhibited. Jehovah is the individual agreement God of Israel, who is in the meantime the God of paradise and earth. The name indicates the unceasing self-presence of the Author of all presence. It is the expressive of God's lovingkindness, his elegance, his leniency, his lordship, and his unceasing relationship to his own particular divinely selected individuals who are made in his picture. Jehovah's exceptional relationship to Israel would be depicted all the more particularly when he would show up at the consuming bramble close Sinar. Here the Author of life is related to the celestial Creator of Genesis 1.

6. "A mist used to go up...and water." with a specific end goal to set up the ground to play out its named work, the Creator provided dampness. The typical interpretation alludes to an exceptionally slight shower of rain, or a fog. It is conceivable that the word deciphered "fog" in the AV ('ed) could be interpreted "waterway"

or "stream." The previous is to be favored. In any occasion, the "fog" was God's method for working out his will for the dirt. Consistent activity is communicated.

7. "The Lord God formed (yasar) man of the dust of the ground." Again the two names for God are participated in expectation of the age making occasion. The word yasar is utilized to give the figure of a potter at work, forming with his hands the plastic material he holds (cf. Jer. 18:3,4).

A similar verb is utilized to picture the forming of a people or a country. Man's body was designed from the tidy of the ground, while his soul originated from the very "breath" of God. He is truly an animal of two universes; both earth and paradise can assert him. Notice the three explanations; "Jehovah shaped" (yasar) "man of the dust".... "Jehovah God inhaled" (napah) "into the nostrils the breath of life."..." man progressed toward becoming" (hayah) "a living soul." The initial step was exceedingly essential, yet the dampened tidy was a long way from being man until the point when the second supernatural occurrence was finished. God imparted his own particular life to that inactive mass of substance he had already made and shaped into frame. The celestial breath pervaded the material and changed it into a living being. That weird blend of tidy and divinity delivered a wonderful creation (cf. I Cor. 15:47-49), made in God's own particular picture. As a living being, man was bound to uncover the characteristics of the Giver of Life.

This dialect of Scripture does not recommend that man looked somewhat like God. Or maybe, he was made like God in otherworldly powers. To him were offered forces to think and feel, to speak with others, to recognize and segregate, and, to a specific degree, to decide his own character.

8. "A garden (gan)....in Eden" (b'eden). The creator speaks to God as planting a lovely garden for his new animals. The word implies a fenced in area or a recreation center. The LXX here utilizations a term that structures the reason for our oath "heaven." Man's work in that garden was to practice domain while serving – a great blend. The obligations most likely were thorough yet pleasant. Eden, or the place that is known for Eden, most likely lay in the lower some portion of the Babylonian valley.

In spite of the fact that many adversary claims for the area of Eden have been propelled, the proof appears to point to the territory between the Tigris and the Euphrates as the support of human progress.

The Hebrew word Eden likely signifies "charm," "joy," or "pleasure." In this peaceful place of incredible magnificence, man was to appreciate association and fraternity with the Creator, and to work as per the celestial diagram to idealize His will. Brilliant trees outfitted supporting sustenance, however man needed to work to tend to them. Sufficient water supply was guaranteed by an immense water system framework, a system of waterways that streamed in and about the garden with its nurturing waters.

To lead man to full good and profound advancement, God gave him particular orders and a particular denial to administer his conduct. He additionally gave him the benefit of developing in divine support. Along these lines started the ethical train of man.

18. "An help meet for him" ('ezer k'negdo). The propelled creator in a roundabout way uncovers man's characteristic dejection and

absence of full fulfillment. In spite of the fact that much had been improved the situation him, yet he was aware of a need. The Creator had not wrapped up. He had plans for giving a companion who might fulfill the unfulfilled desires of man's heart. Made for association and brotherhood, man could go into the full life just as he may share love, trust, and commitment in the private hover of the family relationship. Jehovah made it feasible for man to have "an assistance meet for him." Literally, an assistance offering an explanation to him, or, one who answers. She was to be one who could share man's duties, react to his inclination with comprehension and adore, and wholeheartedly co-work with him in working out the arrangement of God.

21. "Deep sleep (tardema) .... made" her (bana). Today physcians utilize different sedatives to create profound rest. We don't recognize what means or technique the Creator used to initiate in Adam such "profound rest" that he was unaware of the occasions. That remaining parts a puzzle. Surely divine leniency was shown in this marvel. The Eternal was bringing into being another person, as well as another one, very surprising, with another sex.

Somebody has said that "lady was taken not from man's make a beeline for lead over him, nor from man's feet to be trampled upon, yet from his side, under his arm, to be ensured, and nearest his heart, to be adored." She is additionally spoken to in the story of creation as entirely subordinate upon her better half and not finish without him.

So also, man is never completely total without the lady (woman). It is God's will that it ought to be so. Since woman was framed from man's side, she is bound to him and committed to be a "help" to him. He is committed to give her the full assurance and gave protecting of his arm. The two creatures make up the finished entire, the crown of creation. The creator of Genesis announces that God "builded" (bana) the rib which he had taken from man into a lady (woman). The hand that had shaped earth into the material for the assemblage of man remove a portion of the living assortment of man and builded it into a woman.

22. "Brought her unto the man." When God was prepared with this new creation, he "gave her away" in marriage to her better half, hence setting up the interminably critical organization

of marriage. As the Creator established marriage, it was a holy relationship of man and lady (woman), with profound puzzle at its middle announcing its heavenly source. The cherishing heart of God without a doubt cheered in the organization of a relationship that should have been high, perfect, sacred, and wonderful for humanity.

23. "This is now ....flesh of my flesh." The man perceived in this new creation a supernaturally made sidekick who was molded to give every one of that his eager heart would need to complete God's blessed will. "Woman"...(ishsha)... "man" ('ish). These two Hebrew words are much similar, even in sound. The main contrast between them is that the word for "lady" has a female closure. Later dictionaries pronounce that these words are not etymologically related. There is, notwithstanding, no genuine ground for dismissing the prior view that the word for "woman" is gotten from the word for "man."

24. "Therefore doth a man...cleave (dabaq) unto his significant other." The Creator had built up the full reason for monogamous marriage. The considerable Hebrew analyst, Rashi, proclaims that these words are a particular remark by the

Holy Spirit. The last analysis on the union of man and spouse was given by our Lord, when he stated: "For this reason might a man leave his dad and mom, and sever to his better half; and they twain should be one substance: so then they are no more twain, however one tissue. What in this manner God hath combined, let not man put into pieces" (Mark 10:7-9). God arranged that the marriage bond ought to be perpetually constant. "Sever" (dabaq) intends to "stick himself to" his significant other (his own better half). The word for "spouse" is solitary. The man, who is more grounded, is the person who is to "separate." The spouse will be held when the husband applies the sort of adoring force depicted in this verse. Love is solid and persevering. "What God hath consolidated, let not man put into pieces." This is an old articulation, yet it is really God's assertion for every one of our souls today, and dependably.

How wonderful it is that a relationship so precisely depicted hundreds of years prior by Moses should in any case be established in everlasting truth and heavenly pronouncement! The holiness of marriage is established in the very heart of Scriptures, and forever underlined

CHAPTER

THREE

The Temptation And Fall
(3:1-24)

2,3. "The woman said." To conference with the seducer is constantly risky. Unwittingly, the lady was uncovering an eagerness to grapple with the seducer. She didn't have the upside of Jesus' words in Matt. 4:10 and James' rebuke in James 4:7. She was blameless, sincere, and clueless, and no match for the wily opponent. She was unwilling to remain by and see God distorted to redress the serpent's announcement. Be that as it may, she cited God's restriction erroneously, including "touch."

5. "Ye shall be as God" (divine beings). Since Eve had gone into the discussion, the tempter propelled his all the more capable contention. He immediately recommended that man's incredible want to be on a standard with and really like God had been intentionally foiled by divine charge. He accused the Creator of narrow-mindedness and with a malevolent misrepresentation, speaking to him as desirous and unwilling for his animals to have something that would influence them to like the omniscient One. (The word 'Elohim can be interpreted God

or divine beings, since it is plural. The previous is favored).

6. "The woman saw...took...did eat...gave." The solid verbs recount the story strikingly and obviously. Something occurred in the reasoning of the lady. Progressively the organic product went up against new centrality. It was alluring to the eye, attractive to the taste, and effective to give new shrewdness. She stepped into the field of self-trickery. She not just needed nourishment that was scrumptious and alluring, however she was envious of energy. She trusted this organic product would fulfill every one of her wants. The subsequent stage was programmed and quick. "She took... also, ate." The seducer was not required after that minute. Eve took up his work and displayed the all around prescribed organic product to her significant other, and "he ate."

7. "The eyes...were opened (pakah)... they knew." The word pakah pictures a sudden marvel. The guarantee of the seducer was satisfied rapidly; moment observation was given. They saw and knew. However, what they saw was far unique in relation to the blushing picture painted by the serpent. Still, small voice

was inconsiderately stirred. They saw their bareness, otherworldly and also physical. And after that disgrace and dread were conceived. Whenever Adam and Eve understood that they were withdrawn from God, a horrendous dejection overpowered them. Regret and its inescapable agonies took after.

Their loss of confidence had subjected them to all these specialist burdens. They quickly made "cook's garments" or "supports" to give some quantify of disguise as they looked for a solution for their bewilderment, depression, and blame.

8. "The voice of the Lord God....in the cool of the day." (Kol, "voice," is, lit., sound; l'ruah, "cool," is wind or breeze). They may avoid God, yet they couldn't escape him. The cherishing Creator couldn't ignore their rebellion, nor would he be able to leave shuddering heathens in their impactful need. They were his own. His heavenliness must come, dressed with adoration, to look for, find, and judge them. Usually, the approach of God's strides brought them satisfaction. Presently, fear and fear incapacitated them, however the Lord did not approach in thunder nor call brutally.

9. It is anything but difficult to envision the sweetness of the heavenly voice, as it sounded forward through the trees in the stillness of the night, calling, "Where workmanship thou?" obviously God knew where the man and lady were. Be that as it may, he was speaking to them, looking for through delicacy and love to win a good reaction. What's more, he was looking to lead the transgressors tenderly to a full conviction of their wrongdoing. In spite of the fact that Justice was directing the strategy. Kindness was driving. The Judge would render the choice and articulate the sentence.

12. "The woman...gave me of the tree, and I ate." God's inquiries were immediate and abnormally particular. Rather than making full admission and arguing for kindness, Adam and Eve started to offer reasons and pass the duty on to another. The man to some degree heedlessly tossed a piece of the fault back on God-" whom thou gavest...me.

13. The woman, declining to assume liability, cast everything on the serpent. The serpent had no chance to get of passing it on. "Beguile"(d) (hishshiani). The verb passes on the possibility

of duplicity (cf. Paul's utilization of this idea in II Cor.11:3; I Tim. 2:14).

14. "Reviled, "Cursed ('arur) art thou." The Lord singled out the originator and instigator of the enticement for exceptional judgment and corruption. From that minute he should slither in the clean and even eat it. He would crawl his way along in disrespect, and scorn would be coordinated against him from all headings. Man would dependably see him as an image of the corruption of the person who had criticized God (cf. Isa. 65:25).

He was to speak to not only the serpent race, but rather the energy of the malevolent kingdom. For whatever length of time that life proceeded with, men would loathe him and try to demolish him.

15. "I will put hatred (enmity)." The word 'eba means the blood-quarrel that runs most profound in the core of man (cf. Num. 35:19,20; Ezk. 25:15-17; 35:5,6). "Thou shalt wound" (shup). A prediction of a proceeding with battle between the relatives of lady and of the serpent to crush each other. The verb shup is uncommon (cf. Employment 9:17; Ps. 139:11). It is the same in the two provisions. At the point when

deciphered pulverize, it appears to be fitting to the reference concerning the leader of the serpent, yet not exactly so precise in portraying the assault of the serpent on man's foot sole area. It is additionally rendered lie in sit tight for, go for, or (LXX) look for. The Vulgate renders it conteret, "wound," "lie in hold up," in the other condition. Hence, we have in this renowned entry, called the protevangelium, "first gospel," the declaration of a delayed battle, unending enmity, wounds on the two sides, and possible triumph for the seed of lady.

God's guarantee that the head of the serpent was to be smashed indicated forward the happening to the Messiah and ensured triumph. This affirmation fell upon the ears of God's most punctual animals as a favored any expectation of reclamation. A grievous interpretation in the Vulgate changes the pronoun his (v.15c) from the manly to the female, giving spurious help to unwarranted cases concerning "the Blessed Virgin Mary."

16. "Unto the woman he said." For the woman, God anticipated subjection to the man, and enduring. Pregnancy and labor would be gone to by torment. The word 'asvon pictures

both mental and physical torment. Eve would understand her womanly longings and wants, yet not without anguish. As it were, as spouse and mother, she was to be liable to the train of Jehovah. Lady's affection and man's lordship are both exhibited in the striking portrayal. We can't completely fathom the idea of such judgments of the Lord.

17. "Unto Adam he said." Physical hardship, excruciating drudge, disillusioning vexations, and hard battle were delegated as the part of the man, who was certainly decreed a blameworthy heathen. In the past the earth had yielded its deliver effectively and uninhibitedly to man, in awesome wealth. Adam had just to "dress" the garden (2:15) keeping in mind the end goal to make the most of its delectable organic products. In any case, now God articulated an uncommon revile on the ground. From this time forward it would yield its grains and natural products reluctantly. Man would need to buckle down developing the dirt to influence it to deliver life's necessities. Furthermore, he would need to grapple with troublesome thistles and weeds not beforehand in confirm. Drudgery, troubles, and exhaustion would be his every day part.

Adam, and in addition for Eve, sin claimed a substantial toll.

20. "Eve" (hawwd) The Hebrew word needs to do with life, and the verb to which it is connected discusses living. All life it is connected discusses living. All life started with the principal lady. She was the mother of every individual and, along these lines, the mother of every group and individuals. As per the awesome reason, life must go on, despite the fact that the proclamation of death had been talked – "unto the clean thou shalt return (v.19).

22-24a. So "he drove out (garash) the man." An essential and forgiving act. The Lord couldn't permit insubordinate man access to the tree of life. With cherishing care he kept Adam and Eve far from the organic product that woould make them undying and along these lines propagate the appalling condition into which sin had brought them. From the stunning patio nursery he drove them out into an unpleasant wild.

24b. "Cherubims, and a flaring sword (AV). The Hebrew translator, Rashi, asserted that these instruments were "blessed messengers of obliteration," intended to devastate any individual who looked for entrance. Hebrew kerubim demonstrates supernaturally framed assumes that fill in as bearers of the divinity or as exceptional gatekeepers of consecrated things. In one example they are indicated maintaining the royal position on which God sits. In another, they used to depict the fear unapproachability of Jehovah. When all is said in done, their capacity is by all accounts to monitor the sacrosanct residence of God from infringement or contamination. The Tree of life was superbly sheltered with the cherubim standing gatekeeper at the entryway. What's more, corrupt man was sheltered from the damage that could have come to him had he not had the glorious defender.

24c. "The flame of a whirling sword" (mithhapeket). The path once more into Eden was monitored by the cherubim as well as by a spinning sword-like fire. This gave assist affirmation that man would not advance, toward the tree of life. In spite of the fact that man's heaven was shut to him since he had turned into a heathen, Jehovah did not overlook his animals. He had effectively made arrangement for their triumphant return.

CHAPTER

FOUR

The Two Brothers
(4:1-26)

1. Cain (Qayin). "Cain" is generally connected with the Hebrew word qana, "to secure" or "to get." The induction depends on the likeness of sound, as opposed to on fundamental historical background. It may be known as a statement with a double meaning. The real importance of the word potentially got through the Arabic ("a spear" or "a smith"). Eve was excited at the introduction of her child. She shouted, "I have gotten a man."

2. "Abel" (Hebel). The name given to the second child specifies "a momentary breath" or "a vapor." The related Accadian word aplu implies child. Abel was the originator of peaceful life, while Cain took after his dad in the quest for farming.

3,4. "An offering" (minha). Each man conveyed an exceptional present or blessing to Jehovah. No say is made of the holy place or of the place of the religious recognition. The minha, as the people of yore knew it, served to offer thanks, to impact compromise with the Lord, and to go with venerate. This record pictures the principal demonstration of love recorded in mankind's history. For each situation the admirer brought something of his own as an oblation to the Lord.

5a. "The Lord had respect (sha a). The blessing brought by Cain was not gotten by the Lord. No reason is given here for the dismissal. furthermore, the Scripture does not reveal to us how God showed his dissatisfaction. It might be that fire tumbled from paradise and devoured the acknowledged offering however left the other untouched. Some have felt that Cain's putting forth was rejected on the grounds that Cain neglected to play out the best possible custom. Others have propelled the possibility that the idea of the endowments had the effect – the one being fragile living creature and including demise and gore (cf. Heb. 9:22).

The creator of the Epistle to the Hebrews gives us the enlivened clarification of the distinction between the offerings: "By confidence Abel offered unto God a more superb give up than Cain .... God taking the stand regard of his blessings" (Heb. 11:4). This clarification focuses upon the distinction in soul showed by the two men. Since Abel was a man of confidence, he came in the correct soul and introduced revere that satisfied God.

We have motivation to trust that Abel had some acknowledgment of his requirement for substitutionary compensation. To all appearances the two offerings offered thanks, thanksgiving and dedication to God.

Be that as it may, the man who needed authentic confidence in his heart couldn't please God despite the fact that the material blessing was spotless. God did not look upon Cain since He had just taken a gander at him and seen what was in his mind. Abel came to God in the correct state of mind of heart for revere and in the main way corrupt men can approach "a sacred God. Cain did not.

5b. Cain's unbridled outrage showed itself in a flash. Incensed anger bursted out, uncovering the soul that was held up with in the heart. Cain turned into an adversary of God and unfriendly to his sibling. Hence, injured pride delivered envy and a soul of requital. Furthermore, these delivered the consuming disdain and savagery that made murder conceivable.

6,7a. "Countenance fallen....a lifting up." The warmth that bursted inside him made his face "fall." It expedited agonizing and an unattractive, grim soul. Tenderly and quietly God managed Cain, trying to spare the insubordinate delinquent. He guaranteed him that in the event that he would earnestly apologize, he may again lift up his face in satisfaction and compromise. Nasa, "lift up," fits the possibility of absolution. The tolerant Jehovah along these lines held out to Cain the expectation of absolution and triumph as he confronted his pivotal choice.

7b. "Sin" (hatt'at) "coucheth" (rabas). Close upon that delighting guarantee, Jehovah expressed a firm cautioning, encouraging the delinquent to remain calm and be careful keeping in mind that a squatting brute (sin) spring upon him and eat up him. The threat was genuine. The fatal monster was even right then and there prepared to overwhelm him. God's statement requested moment activity and solid push to shock the future winner. Cain must not let these bubbling considerations and motivations drive him to ruinous conduct. God made his solid interest to Cain's will. The will must be over transgression (hat'at) finish.

It was dependent upon Cain to vanquish sin in himself, to control instead of be controlled.

The snapshot of fate had arrived. It was not very late for him to pick the method for God.

9. "Where is Abel thy brother?" Failing to pick up authority over the savage creature, Cain soon ended up helpless before a power that controlled him totally. Very quickly one child turned into a killer and the other a saint. Jehovah came rapidly to face the killer with an inquiry. Apparently, he wanted to inspire an admission of blame that could set up the route for benevolence and full acquit.

In spite of the fact that Cain had unyieldingly trespassed, he got himself sought after by an adoring God, rich in effortlessness. "Am I my sibling's manager?" (shomer) A despicable reaction to an inquiry from a cherishing Father (God)! Petullaantly, disobediently, Cain made his answer. Sin as of now had him in the grasp of a tight clamp. He repudiated the clamant privileges of fraternity. He declined to indicate regard to the interminable God. He shamelessly reclined without anyone else narrow minded resistance and talked what nobody should set out to absolute.

10. "The voice (qol) of the bloods of thy brother are crying (soqim) unto me starting from

the earliest stage." spilled by a killer, however secured by earth, was shouting out to God. Jehovah could hear it, and he comprehended the significance of the cry, for he knew about Cain's blame. How mournfully those "bloods" were shouting out for retribution! The creator of Hebrews alludes to this involvement in the expression, "the blood of sprinkling that speaketh preferable things over that of Abel" (12:24).

12. "A fugitive (na) and a wanderer" (nad). The revile articulated on the killer included expulsion from nourishment creating soil to the inefficient forsake. The ground, God stated, would be threatening to the killer, with the goal that he couldn't get sustenance from working the dirt. In his look for subsistence, he would turn into a Bedouin of the waste terrains, meandering about in exhaustion and sadness.

Frailty, eagerness, hard battle, blame, and fears, were to obe his steady "partners." The word for "criminal" conveys tottering, stunning, faltering uncertainly along in an unproductive scan for fulfillment. It was a terrible, debilitating prospect.

13. "My punishment" (awon). Despite the fact that Cain's life was saved, he trembled under the heaviness of his wrongdoing, his blame, his discipline, and the unending results that lingered before him, The Hebrew word awon truly alludes to his evildoing, however it additionally contains the prospect of the outcomes of his transgression.

Cain was much more worried about his sentence than with his transgression. "More prominent than I can endure." His intense cry to God pointed out the insufferable weight of his discipline. It was heavier than he could lift and convey. The Hebrew word nasa conveys the thoughts of "taking ceaselessly" (pardoning) and "lifting up" (appeasement). Once more, it appears to be certain that the startled killer was pondering to happen upon him.

14b. "Every one....shall slay me." Dread and melancholy begin to overpower the wicked man as the possibility of the hazards of the betray. He envisioned that pitiless adversaries would joy to slaughter him. He could feel the hot breath of the justice fighter on his neck. His dynamic still, small voice was at that point at work. In his dread, he was certain that specific pulverization anticipated him, for he felt that he would be totally outside the hover of God's care.

15. "A sign (ot) for Cain." But Jehovah, in benevolence, guaranteed Cain of his proceeding with nearness and unending insurance. He set a "sign" on him – obviously a stamp or assignment to demonstrate that Cain had a place with the Lord God and must be saved substantial damage. There is no proof that the characteristic of Cain' was an indication to report to the world that he was a killer.

It was, fairly, an uncommon sign of cherishing consideration and insurance. Cain would proceed dependably in the protection of the contract God. In spite of the fact that a killer, he was the beneficiary of God's support.

16. "Place of Nod" (gesture). Truly, place where there is meandering or flight (cf. 4:12,14). There is no real way to find this zone geologically but to talk about it as being "east of Eden." Cain was yet satisfying the forecast God made concerning his future presence. Pitifully and stoically he set out into the trackless squanders. The thoughts of "flight" and "wretchedness" are noticeable in the Hebrew word for "went out."

17. "His wife" (ishto). The Book of Genesis does not answer the oft-rehashed question: Where did Cain get his significant other? It makes it clear that numerous different children and girls were destined to Adam and Eve. It additionally introduces the slip by of numerous years (possibly many years) previously Cain's marriage encounter. Since all life originated from the primary supernaturally made human combine, it is important to reason that sooner or later siblings and sisters were hitched to each other. When Cain was prepared to set up a home, Adam and Eve had various relatives.

It is not in any manner important to envision another race of individuals officially settled on the planet. Cain's better half was one of the group of Adam and Eve.

25. "Seth" (Shet). The heavenly story has safeguarded the name "Seth" as that of the third child in Adam's line. The Hebrew word indicates checked comparability to the word crapped, deciphered "selected" or "set." In actuality, Seth turned into the one on whom God could depend as the establishment stone for His family. He was "set" or "delegated" to take up the work and mission of Abel.

CHAPTER

FIVE

Seth And His Descendants
(5:1-32)

22. "Enoch" (Hanok) walked with God." Into a story of birth and horrid presence and possible demise, the creator all of a sudden presents a brilliant character, Enoch, who satisfied the Lord and lived in his quick nearness. In a breaking down age, Enoch an amazing exhibit of admirable devotion. In thought, word, deed, and state of mind he was as per the celestial will; and he conveyed satisfaction to the core of his Maker.

The LXX says in regards to him: "Enoch was well-satisfying unto God." One striking explanation uncovers a trace of the start of Enoch's stroll with God (cf. 22a). It might have been right now of the introduction of his child kid, without a doubt a high minute in his life, that he set his heart on imply fellowship with his God. He close relationship in such environment brought him glorious intelligence, which fitted him to comprehend and value the rich things of God.

24. "He was not; for God took him." because of his authentic devotion and his anxiety of

awesome astuteness, he was lifted from the earth to proceed with his stroll in the holy areas past. His vanishing was sudden and completely unannounced, and passing had nothing to do with it. The LXX says: with respect to him: He was not found, for God interpreted him.

"By faith Enoch was interpreted," says the author of Hebrews, "that he ought not see demise, and he was not found, since God had deciphered him (Heb. 11:5). A wonderful and significant supernatural occurrence was fashioned so the limited who had figured out how to love God and stroll with him may proceed in that fellowship without interruption.

CHAPTER

SIX

Sin And The Flood
(6:1-8:22)

2. "The sons of God (b'ne 'Elohim) .... daughters of men." Wickedness was expanding on each hand. Cain's relatives turned out to be exceedingly heathen and agnostic. A capable race of goliaths, call "Nephilim," became a force to be reckoned with. The verb napal, to fall, has been viewed as the wellspring of the thing, thus these huge animals have been thought of as "fallen ones." The reference to the b'ne 'Elohim has occasioned stamped contrasts of assessment among researchers. 'Elohim is plural in shape. It is generally interpreted "God." But it can be deciphered "divine beings," as, for example, when it alludes to the lords of the rapscallion neighbors of Israel.

It can, likewise, signify the sublime hover of creatures in close association with Jehovah, occupants of paradise, allocated particular obligations as God's colleagues (see Job 1:6). At times in Scripture "children of God" might be related to "heavenly attendants" or "flag-bearers." Jesus is the Son of God in a novel sense.

Devotees are called "children of God" due to their relationship to him. In the Old Testament, in any case, children of God are an exceptional class of creatures that make up the glorious court.

The reference to the relational unions of b'ne 'Elohim to the girls of men has been managed from numerous points of view. To interpret it truly would influence the entry to state that individuals from the superb organization chose decision ladies from the earth and set up marriage associations with them, truly and really.

This can be the main understanding of Job 1:6. There, the b'ne 'Elohim were obviously the individuals from God's grand court. This is the main true blue and right sense that can be acknowledged (S.R. Driver, 1948). Jesus' answer to the Sadducces, in Matt. 22:30, appears to make this view untenable. He said that the holy messengers "neither wed nor are given in marriage." The announcement in Gen. 6:2 influences it to clear that lasting marriage is depicted. Ladies were picked and compelled to end up gatherings to the unnatural relationship. Book of scriptures understudies who have rejected this arrangement have turned to different clarifications. Some have said that a union Seth's virtuous line with Cain's pagan relatives is depicted.

Still others hold that these words allude to marriage between people of high society of society and those of a lower or less commendable class. In the light of the certainties and the precise rendering of the expressions of the content, we reason that a few men of the wonderful gathering (heavenly attendants or errand people) really took spouses of the natural ladies. They utilized better power than overwhelm them, to influence the victory to finish. The "children of God" were powerful (cf. II Pet. 2:4; Jude 6).

3. "My spirit (ruah) might not generally endeavor (yadon) with (or act in) man." This Hebrew verb might be deciphered either endeavor with or reside in. The main interpretation utilizing power on defiant man to hold him in line and to keep him from absolute decimation because of his evil conduct. The second view would speak to God as resolved to pull back the essential breath of life from man, with the outcome, obviously, that passing would result. The Hebrew word dun (or clamor)

demonstrates life communicating in real life or in confirmations of energy.

In the primary translation, the "soul" (ruah) is viewed as a moral standard used to limit or to control the made one, the outcome being moral conduct. In the other, the "soul" (ruah) is viewed as an indispensable rule given to the lifeless piece of mud to give life, inspiration, and power for living.

At the point when that ruah is pulled back by the celestial hand, judgment is finished. This awesome declaration originated from commanded by transgression. It is God's revelation that he should forsake man to the fate of death. Sin had gotten under way that which would ensure passing.

5,6. "Wickedness (ra at)....repented (naham).... lamented ('asab). The debasement was boundless. Also, it was internal, nonstop, and ongoing. Man was completely degenerate, terrible in heart and in direct. There was no great in him. The entire bowed of his considerations and creative abilities was totally out of line with the will of Jehovah.

Substance was on the position of royalty. God was overlooked or transparently opposed. Naham in the niphal shape portrays the adoration for God that has endured shocking dissatisfaction. Truly, it talks about taking a full breath in outrageous agony. God's motivations and plans had neglected to create the valuable natural product that he had foreseen, in light of the fact that corrupt man had kept their full fulfillment.

Asab in the hithpael frame intends to puncture oneself or to encounter penetrating. The announcement says, at that point, that God experienced heart-penetrating distress as he looked upon the lamentable annihilation sin had delivered. His handicraft had been defaced and demolished. Through everything, God's adoration shone obviously, notwithstanding when the thunderings of awesome judgment started to debilitate the general population of the earth.

7. "Blot out" (maha; AV, decimate). The verb shows a development that wipes wipe or scratches out totally. The operation was intended to pulverize each living thing that hindered. Full demolition was to be executed. Nothing was to be saved.

8. "But Noah found grace (hen). One man of all the incalculable hoards then on the earth

was fit to get God's endowment of beauty. "Grace" positively signifies "support" or "acknowledgment," at any rate, and most likely has a considerably wealthier importance. It was love and leniency in real life. God's stretching out beauty to Noah meant that there was new life and new seek after humanity in the near future.

9. "Noah was a righteous man and perfect.... also, Noah walked with God." With these words the creator depicts three qualities of a virtuous life – equity, immaculateness, and heavenliness (cf. 6:8-he discovered elegance according to the Lord).

"Righteous," from Hebrew saddig, depicts Noah's character as it showed itself in connection to other people. "Straightness" or "uprightness" was obvious in his conduct. The majority of his direct this good and moral nobility (cf. Ezk. 14:14, 20). Hebrew tamim, "culminate," portrays the idealized result of an insightful manufacturer; it is full, total, and faultless. Seen equitably, the word faultless portrays character.

In the domain of morals, the possibility of "honesty" turns out as the determined significance (cf. Employment 1:1). The announcement, "he strolled with God," opens another territory of thought. In strolling with God, Noah had shown a soul, a state of mind and character that made him acknowledged and endorsed for the most close otherworldly relationship. He showed characteristics of soul that charmed him to the Lord (cf. Gen. 5:22; Mic. 6:8; Mal. 2:6).

14-16. "An Ark" (teba). The English word "Ark" descended through the Latin arca, "a chest or coffer." The word for the "ark" of the agreement is an alternate word – 'aron. Teba is most likely of Egyptian inception. Noah's ark was likely a sort of extensive secured pontoon worked of light resinous wood,. It was four hundred and fifty feet long and seventy-five feet wide.

Cells, homes, or little rooms, were worked at the edges of the three stories. To make the specialty watertight, an effective "pitch," or bitumen, was utilized inside and outside, as a calking compound. The Hebrew word sohar can best be deciphered a light or window. This was roughly eighteen creeps in stature and expanded totally around the ark; it conceded light and air.

17-22. "Flood" (mabbul). This word has no Hebrew historical underpinnings. It was utilized just of the downpour of Noah. It might have originated from Assyrian nabalu, "to devastate." According to the creator of Genesis, God's motivation was positively to convey to an end the living things of his creation.

Amid the 120 years while Noah was finishing his work, he was lecturing the general population in a critical push to make them atone. They saw the ark come to fruition before their eyes while the minister conveyed his sermons. Noah's close family, including his significant other, his three children, and their spouses, went with him into the asylum to security. In submission to God's charge, they brought with them agent sets of the considerable number of creatures of the earth.

CHAPTER

SEVEN

Sin And The Flood
(7-8:22)

11a,b. "The fountains of the great deep (were) broken up (baqa). Huge supplies of water were put away under the earth. This relentless accumulation of waters was called t'hom, "the immense profound" (cf. Gen 1:2). These underground waters, kept by inventive power on the second day of creation, were released to pour forward in volume and in savagery resisting depiction.

It was not a customary surge, but rather a mammoth tsunami that broke all of a sudden upon a startled people. Baqa shows an earthly shaking that split in half every controlling obstruction that had existed. It was a wild loosening up of unbelievable obliteration.

Man can't envision the wrath and the dangerous may of the ejection, nor the horrendousness of the show of God's energy to annihilate corrupt creatures. The total debasement of men was far more awful than any of us can envision. The annihilation was fundamental.

11c, 12. "The windows of the heaven were opened" (patah). Notwithstanding the dynamite change from underneath, the people groups of the earth saw the opening of the entryways of the powerful supplies of waters over the earth. All the put away waters burst forward in deluges. Resistlessly and ceaselessly for forty days and forty evenings, the monstrous downpour poured downward on the earth. The impact of the downpour on men, ladies, kids, creatures, and plants, and the world's surface can't be totally envisioned.

16-18. "The Lord shut him in (sagar).....And the waters won (gabar). Amidst the furious tempest and the flooding deluges, Jehovah, the contract God, connected a hand of kindness and close the entryway of the ark to guard his kin. In any case, he poured forward deluges of water to pulverize totally the miscreants on earth.

The tenants of the gliding house could ride the waters with a suspicion that all is well and good and supervision, for they put stock in God. The perfect hand that had separated the profound and opened the windows of the sky to spill out annihilation had additionally shown

God's adoring worry for the individuals who were to be the core for his fresh start.

While God's divinely selected individuals settled securely in the ark, the waters kept on expanding and to assume control over the earth. The verb gabar demonstrates authority, subjection, and winning force. Perseveringly the waters took control and kept on being in charge until the point that the high mountains were totally submerged. Once more, the loftiness, may, and convincing reason for the Almighty turned out to be progressively obvious. The awesome reason for existing was being worked out in all the earth. God's will was being proficient.

CHAPTER

EIGHT

Sin And The Flood
(8:4-22)

4. "The mountains of Ararat." Following 150 days, the ark endless supply of the pinnacles of the high ranges in Armenia. Urantu, Accadian related of "Ararat, is utilized as a part of antiquated records to assign Armenia. The mountain now called Ararat towers to the stature of 16, 916 feet.

The Babylonian surge story, a piece of the Gilgamesh Epic, relates how its saint, similar to the Biblical Noah, constructed an ark, brought into it examples of the set of all animals, and, after the surge arrived on Mount Nisir east of the Tigris River.

20. "Noah built an altar (mizbeah) to Jehovah." As Noah moved out into the splendid new day, the most regular thing for him to do was to locate a high spot of ground and fabricate a mizbeah. It was the primary sacrificial table based on the rinsed earth. Noah perceived the finish of the heartbreaking judgment and the unfolding of another day of expectation and guarantee. Building the holy place was his turn to spill out to Jehovah acclaim and thanksgiving.

"He presented burnt offerings ('ola). The word for "consumed offerings" is gotten from the verb 'alahk, "to go up." The proposal here is that, as the give up was expended, the exhaust went upward to God, bearing it might be said, the appreciation and love of the offerer. It was a genuinely propitiatory give up (cf. II Sam. 24:25), offered in genuine love, out of profound gratefulness. Thus the interminable God was satisfied. Noah had found favor in his eyes.

CHAPTER

NINE

Noah's Later Life, And His Descendants
(9:1-10:32)

9-15. "I established (meqim) my covenant.... I do set (natan) my bow in the mists." In serious way Jehovah affirmed the contract guarantees the had effectively given. The framing of a pledge includes the serious restricting together of two gatherings, until now free from commitment to each other. God's coupling himself to this one family bunch was a deliberate demonstration of free elegance. Noah and his family had done nothing to justify the pledge connection, and God was not committed to them.

Moreover, this was an agreement with all humanity. By tolerating the terms and getting to be noticeably faithful, man bound himself to his Creator to keep the heavenly terms and to watch their internal soul.

The contract need an outward and noticeable sign or "token" as a steady indication of the hallowed understanding. This sign ('ot) would be a vow of the inward profound bond, ensuring its unending dependability. The Hebrew immaculate tense can be deciphered I have set, or I now right now do set.

The bow in the cloud was to be the "sign." God could have made the rainbow right then and there and contributed it with this importance. It is likely, be that as it may, that he indicated the bow as of now in the cloud and demonstrated that it would now go up against new importance, giving confirmation of his kindness and effortlessness; it would be a noticeable indication of his affection. He stated: I will "remember" (v.15).

18. "Shem, Ham, Japheth." The creator of Genesis influences it to clear that these three children of Noah turned into the fathers of the three incredible groups of humanity. "Shem" is named first as involving the place of authority and noticeable quality in God's gets ready for the general population. The Semites (Shemites) were to be profound pioneers of men.

God's anointed ones of that line would educate the religion of Jehovah to the world. We realize that the Messiah was to originate from Shem's relatives. "Japheth" was to be the father of one expansive branch of the Gentile world. His relatives would diffuse far and wide in their look for material pick up and control.

They would be prosperous and exceedingly intense. "Ham" was to be the father of the other branch of Gentiles, including Egyptians, Ethiopians, Abyssinians, and related gatherings. His child, Canaan, turned into the father of the gatherings called Canaanites, the tenants of the place where there is Canaan, later confiscated by the Hebrews. The revile articulated upon Canaan by Noah was not, in any sense, composed as a proof content in servitude or isolation exchanges.

CHAPTER

TEN

Noah's Later Life, And His Descendants (10:4-32)

4. "Tarshish." The celebrated around the world city in Spain to which the Phoenician brokers went. Hundreds of years after the fact the prophet Jonah boarded a ship destined for that far off city. The Greeks called it Tartessus.

6. "Mizraim." The right Hebrew word for Egypt, involving the lower and the upper divisions of that land. The two capitals of Egypt were Memphis and Thebes.

8,9. "Nimrod." Son of Cush. He established the early Babylonian realm and constructed the city of Nineveh. He was a powerful seeker and a noteworthy pioneer of armed forces. His energy reached out finished the urban areas of Mesopotamia.

11,12. "Nineveh." Known as ahead of schedule as 2800 B.C., it was the focal point of the capable Assyrian kingdom, which achieved its stature under Sennacherib, Esarhaddon, and Ashurbanipal. It was arranged on the Tigris River, around 250 miles from the city of Babylon. It was against this fortress that Jonah and Nahum coordinated their predictions.

14. "The Philistines" (cf. AV Philistim) are attributed with having given their name to the place where there is "Palestine." Amos and Jeremiah allude to them as originating from Captor. Their five main urban areas were Ashdod, Ashkelon, Gaza, Gath, and Ekron. The Philistines proceeded for a considerable length of time to be a thistle in the tissue of the Israelites.

15. "Heth." Ancestor of the Hittites, whose incredible domain held influence from 1600-700 B.C. The chief urban areas of the Hittites were Carchemish on the Euphrates and Kadesh on the Orontes. These individuals settled in the region of Hebron, and saw Abraham's buy of the Cave of Machpelah from Ephron (23:8-10).

Esau wedded into the tribe. The Hittites discovered their way into the Assyrian and Egyptian engravings. Archeologists have discovered profitable stays of the progress of that intense realm.

21. "The children of Eber" contained various gatherings among the children of Shem. The name "Eber" has been related with the word Hebrew, the name by which the Israelites were known by different people groups.

They were the ones who had the information of the genuine God. The expression "Hebrew" is racial, while "Israellite" is national. In later days, these words were utilized as equivalent words.

22. "Aram," or the Aramean or Syrian individuals, made up the gathering around and inside Damascus. They figured noticeably in the historical backdrop of the general population of Israel. The Aramaic dialect turned into the dialect of exchange and discretionary relations. It step by step dislodged the Hebrew dialect until, at the season of our Lord, Aramaic was the dialect of discussion and composing.

28. "Sheba" is frequently said in the Old Testament to mean a rich gathering of individuals whose main work was to outfit gold, aromas, and valuable stones for fare to Palestine and to Egypt. They are related to the Sabaeans, who held an unmistakable place in exchange and in legislative accomplishment. So far as Bible understudies are concerned, the ruler of Sheba was the most acclaimed of the general population of Sheba.

29. "Ophir" was really popular for its fine gold. Solomon sent his men alongside Hiram's

to extricate it and to transport it to Palestine. Notwithstanding gold, they discovered valuable metals and diamonds in extraordinary wealth. Before long Solomon's kingdom matched all the encompassing terrains in riches.

Ophir was presumably a seaport on the shoreline of Arabia. It has been situated as far away as the mouth of the Indus. A significant part of the gold overlay of the Temple of Solomon originated from Ophir.

CHAPTER
ELEVEN

The Tower Of Babel
(11:1-32)

1,2. "The whole earth was of one language." Beginning pictures Noah and his children approaching from the ark having one dialect and one arrangement of words. As the relatives of Noah increased, they normally proceeded with that same dialect, since it was adequate. They lived in and about the Euphrates valley, the area typically viewed as the support of human progress.

"Shinar." The Hebrews utilized the name Shinar, initially a locale in northern Mesopotamia, to assign the entire area of Mesopotamia. Moving wanderers moved along the mountains of Ararat to the very much watered fields of Babylonia.

3,4. "Let us build a city....a tower .... and... make us a name." When Noah's eastbound moving relatives had discovered a spot where they could start perpetual base camp, they chose to fabricate a city. They would build a huge pinnacle so high that its best would puncture the "vault" above them.

This incredible structure would give them the place of vantage by which they could set up their significance according to men, and even in God's sight.

The motivation behind the endeavor was twofold. Initially, they needed to guarantee themselves of the quality that originates from solidarity. The city and the pinnacle would tie them into a strong gathering, so they may be effective even without God's assistance.

They stated: "For fear that we be scattered." On the other hand, they were resolved to make themselves famous "make for ourselves a name." The transgressions of independence and pride prevailed in their reasoning. They needed to ensure that they would not be overlooked. The pinnacle would hold them together and secure their names from blankness.

They opposed God and set out to demonstrate their independence. Their transcending structure would be a landmark to their vitality, brave, virtuoso, and assets. many transcending urban communities, for example, Babylon, Sodom, Gomorrah, Sidon, Tire, and Rome, have demonstrated anything besides genuine structures. At the point when men spurn

God's law and effortlessness, and commend themselves, calamity unavoidably falls upon them.

7-9. "Confounded their language." Jehovah comprehended the soul, the thought process, and the egotistical plans of the insubordinate individuals. Instantly he set out to agitate their silly plans. The very thing they had looked to keep away from came abruptly upon them. God straightforwardly interceded to make sure that nobody comprehended the expressions of the others about him.

What's more, he scattered them far and wide. Hebrew balal, "bewilder," demonstrates that there was a particular aggravation that left the general population enormously confounded. "Babel" is interpreted Babylon. The best Hebrew etymologists guarantee that it couldn't have originated from the Hebrew balal, to "confound" or "blend," however that it signified "entryway of God." Through a figure of speech it came to signify "disarray." The Aramaic word balbel signifies "perplexity."

We are helped that the bestowal to remember the endowment of tongues at Pentecost (Acts 2:5-11) can be thought of as the turn around of the perplexity of tongues at Babel. Richardson says: "When men in their pride gloat of their own accomplishments, there comes about only division, perplexity, and immeasurability; yet when the brilliant works of God are declared, at that point each man may hear the biblical gospel in his own particular tongue" (Richardson, 1953).

27. "Terah." Son of Nahor (a relative of Seth) and the father of Abram, Haran, and Nahor. His initial home was in Ur of the Chaldees, however he spent the later years of his life in Haran, where he passed on.

28. "Ur of the Chaldees." An old city of the early Sumerian kingdom, situated around 125 miles from the present mouth of the Euphrates, 100 miles southeast of Babylon, 830 miles from Damascus, and 550 miles from Haran.

It was the capital of Sumer. In Abram's day it was a flourishing commerical city, with strangely high social models. The structures of the sanctuary range were generally intricate. The occupants worshiped the moon-god, Sin. Archeologists have uncovered remarkable fortunes from this old city. The regal graveyard has surrendered craftsmanship treasures dated as ahead of schedule as 2900 B.C.

The Oriental Institute of Chicago has a plaque from Ur that goes back to 3000 B.C. It was in this antiquated world that Abraham was conceived and developed into masculinity. His was a rich legacy.

31. "Haran" (or Harran). A critical city in old Mesopotamia. it was arranged around 500 miles upper east of Ur and 280 miles nor of Damascus. Guideline courses met there. Thruways to Nineveh, Babylon, and Damascus had their begin from it. It was just 60 miles from the fortification of Carrchemish, the capital of the Hittite domain.

Haran was one of the main habitats for the love of Sin, the moon-god. Terah and his family moved to Haran, and the record expresses that Terah passed on there. Rebekah, the spouse of Isaac, and Rachel, the wife of Jacob, experienced childhood in Haran. Despite everything it gets by as a little Arab town.

CHAPTER

TWELVE

The Patriarchs:
(12:1-50:26)

Abraham
(12:1-25:18)

In the second main division of the Book of Genesis, it is obvious that in the new request of things God's divinely selected individuals must perceive the immediate correspondence and the immediate authority of the Lord. In parts 12-50 four characters emerge as men who heard God's voice, comprehended his headings, and requested their courses as per his will.

The reason for Jehovah was still to raise up a people who might complete his will in the earth. In Noah he had made another begin. Shem was the one conveyed forward genuine religion. The Semites (relatives of Shem) were to wind up evangelists to alternate people groups of the earth.

In part 12 Abram starts to rise up out of the line of Shem as Jehovah's picked agent. On him Jehovah would put the full duty of accepting and passing on His disclosure for all. From the agnostic foundation of Ur and Haran approached God's man for the vital hour of early Old Testament disclosure.

1. And Jehovah said, Get thee out of thy country, and from thy kindred, and from thy father's house. The Biblical record influences it to clear that before moving to Palestine, Abram had two homes. He spent his initial a very long time in Ur and after that a long season in Haran. Every people group turned into his home. He needed to leave companions, neighbors, and related behind him when he cleared out Ur and still others when he left from Haran, For each situation, the triple tie of land, individuals, and related was disjoined.

Abram was charged "(a) to revoke the convictions of the past, (b) to confront vulnerabilities without bounds, (c) to search for and take after the bearing of Jehovah's will" (Ryle, 1914). It was a major request (cf. Heb. 11:8). Extreme trials anticipated him. This call more likely than not come to him while regardless he lived in Ur (Acts 7:2). It was reestablished numerous years after the fact in Haran.

"Unto the land that I will show thee." Jehovah did not name the land as of now nor depict it.

In this manner, Abram was to meet another trial of confidence. The Lord had discovered the man for his motivation, one he could subject to overwhelming strains, a man who might respect the doing of God's will as the one vital thing in his life.

2,3. "Be thou a blessing" (b'raka). The basic shape really communicates a result "with the goal that thou shalt be a gift." This recognized voyager from polytheistic Mesopotamia had been supernaturally appointed to go forward into the middle of absolute outsiders in some new land. He and his relatives would constitute a channel by which God would favor every one of the people groups of the world.

"I will make of thee a great nation, and I will bless thee, and make thy name great." God unequivocally strengthened Abram with pledge guarantees of success, plenteous descendants, and significance. The guarantee of awesome gift ensured Abram all that he could want. His each need would be provided.

Indeed, even unfriendly neighbors would come to look upon him as the pioneer of God's kin. Through him would come endowments to all people groups of the earth. Furthermore, his name would be regarded and worshipped all over.

Today, Abram is perceived and regarded as a "father" by Christians, Jews, and Moslems. God picked Abram and his relatives to endure His Gospel to the world. From the line of Abram, Christ was to come, to satisfy God's motivations. What's more, through "conceived once more" men and ladies, His beliefs were to discover satisfaction. The arrangement of God was coming to fruition.

5. "The land of Canaan." Abram deciphered the call of God to include prompt flight for Canaan. How he knew Canaan was his goal is not clarified. Be that as it may, God had stated: "Get thee out....unto a land that I will indicate thee." So he complied. Decisively he assembled his family and set out on a noteworthy movement. Apparently he had no feelings of trepidation, no questions, no doubts.

He ventured to Carchemish on the Euphrates and turned south through Hamath to Damascus of Syria. Josephus speaks to Abram amid his stay in that capital city as acting in the limit of a lord over the general population of Damascus. The place that is known for Canaan is depicted in Scripture as containing all the land from the Jordan to the Mediterranean and from Syria to Egypt.

Moab and Edom limited it on the southeast. In the Bible "Canaanites" typically alludes to the soonest occupants of the land, including any gathering that lived there before the happening to the Hebrews.

6. "Shechem." This old city was most likely a holy place or consecrated place. It was an essential settlement at the intersection of the fundamental business interstates. It was arranged between Mount Gerizim and Mount Ebal, around forty-one miles north of Jerusalem. In later years, Jacob's well was in the prompt region. In later circumstances, Shechem has been called Nablus.

Abram advanced toward the "terebinth of Moreh. This was presumably a consecrated tree, under which a minister or instructor or diviner gave his direction or educating. "Moreh" is most likely a participle of the verb yara, "to educate." The oak and the terebinth trees looked like each other. Shechem turned into Abram's first vital stop in Canaan. Here he got an extraordinary message of affirmation and guarantee from the Lord.

God gave the land to him as his ownership, and guaranteed that his relatives would have it after him. With warlike tribes on each hand, Abram would think that its hard to set up his cases to the new land. He made a decent start, be that as it may, by promptly setting up a holy place and offering penances to Jehovah.

as his life fit as a fiddle, he announced his articulate reliance upon the Lord and his entire hearted commitment to him.

8. Bethel (Bet-el). This old haven goes back to the twenty-first century B.C., and is specified more regularly in Scripture than some other city with the exception of Jerusalem. It is arranged headed straight toward Shechem, around ten or eleven miles north of Jerusalem. by raising a sacrificial stone, the patriarch broadcasted his faithfulness to Jehovah, and by pitching his tents, he freely pronounced to all onlookers that he was taking lasting ownership of the land.

In these two emblematic acts, Abram uncovered his steadfast confidence in the energy of Jehovah of hosts to complete every one of His guarantees. "Bethel" implies, truly, place of God. A later story shows that Jacob gave the place that name after his involvement with Jehovah there (28:19). Abram "approached the name of Jehovah." In his demonstration of honest to goodness revere, he utilized the name Jehovah in the summon (cf.4:26).

9. "Abram journeyed" (nasa) going toward the Negeb. Nasa intends to cull or draw up tent pins. It alludes to Abram's setting out for the south. He pulled up stakes and moved by simple stages.

The Negeb, dry land, is an unmistakable area of southern Palestine, between Kadesh-barnea and Beer-sheba. in the mid year it was sufficiently dry to be a betray, without water or vegetation. With every one of his rushes and groups, Abram thought that it was important to have a lot of water and grass. The Negeb would be of little help to him.

The Patriarch In Egypt
(12:10-20)

10. "And Abram went down into Egypt to sojourn there." Famines were visit in Canaan. Nothing should be possible to forestall them.

The one cure was to move into Egypt, where the Nile outfitted water for steers and products.

Abram and his vast gathering advanced toward Egypt. The Hebrew word gar, "visit," demonstrates that a transitory habitation was foreseen. When the starvation had loosed its hold, Abram would be en route back to Palestine. No confirmation is given to help figure out which Pharaoh was deciding in Egypt around then.

11-16. Fear grasped at the core of the patriarch when he drew close to the royal residence of the ruler. He envisioned that the Pharaoh would look to murder him keeping in mind the end goal to take Sarai into his array of mistresses. In like manner, Abram concocted the arrangement of passing his significant other off as his sister, calming his still, small voice in the mean time with the possibility that she was his relative.

It was a despicable catalyst to utilize. Accordingly, the mother of future pioneers of the Hebrew country was taken into an Egyptian collection of mistresses!

17-20. To settle the entire issue, the Pharaoh was harassed with plagues until the point that he understood that something wasn't right, and drove the guests from the land. Abram excessively Sarai, his adherents, and his property-extraordinarily expanded by his visit in Egypt-and advanced back over the miles to the Negeb and on into Canaan.

Such conduct as Abram's in Egypt was not in the slightest degree deserving of the grand soul of Jehovah's exceptional envoy to the countries. He would need to develop if he somehow managed to estimated the awesome outline for his life. He expected to backpedal to Bethel and reconstruct the sacrificial stone of Jehovah.

CHAPTER

THIRTEEN

The Parting With Lot
(13:1-18)

1-4. "And Abram went up out of Egypt." At the point when the restoration of his partnership with God had been accomplished, Abraham was prepared for another life. He was massively rich. Dairy cattle, gold, and silver were his in awesome wealth. His organization of adherents had expanded until the point that a significant issue stood up to him. With so may steers and sheep, he should have the capacity to move rapidly to secure adequate water and grass.

5-8. Before long Lot's organization experienced issues with Abram's band. Hebrew m'riba, "strife," demonstrates debating, endeavoring, and conflicts. The noble uncle couldn't enable such unbecoming behavior to proceed. He stated: "We are brethren" (v.8). Conduct like that was pointless, unavailing, and entirely out of keeping with God's delegates.

9-13. In light of a legitimate concern for peace and amicability, Abram made the liberal recommendation that Lot pick any area of the land he favored and move toward that path, leaving whatever is left of the domain to Abram.

The narrow minded and getting a handle on nature of Lot showed itself quickly; he picked the very much watered valley of the Jordan.

There, tropical vegetation proliferated under the nurturing waters of the stream. The valley (kiker) of the Jordan was sufficiently extensive and adequately fruitful to ensure thriving and bounty for all the days ahead. In any case, the refers to of Sodom and Gomorrah were incorporated into the range Lot picked, and they were greatly degenerate.

How could otherworldly religion develop among the thistles of narrow-mindedness and debasement in that place? Part's decision turned out to be an awful one. "He set up his portable shelter toward Sodom (v.12). At first he looked toward Sodom. At that point he set up his portable shelter toward Sodom. Later he stayed in Sodom. These are the means by which the man and his family advanced toward certain degeneration and pulverization.

14-17. "And the Lord said unto Abram.... Lift up now thine eyes." In this surprising correspondence, Lot and Abram are set in coordinate complexity. The feeble, narrow minded, getting a handle on heathen decided for himself that which he considered the more significant ownership.

Jehovah decided for Abram. As a reward for his uncommon unselfishness, the patriarch got the place where there is Canaan.

God gave him the title deed to the land and welcomed him to open wide his eyes and devour upon the fortunes that extended before him toward each path. From the slope close Bethel, he could look upon awesome displays of stunning magnificence. They were all his! To make the blessing more alluring, the Lord guaranteed Abram numerous relatives, more various than the sands of the ocean. This prediction more likely than not flabbergasted the patriarch, who had no child. However, he acknowledged it by confidence.

18. "Hebron." An antiquated city in southern Judah, nineteen miles southwest of Jerusalem, at the intersection of all the main thruways of the area. it emerged unmistakably on the scene, 3,040 feet above ocean level. Josephus talks about it as being more antiquated than the city of Memphis in Egypt. He additionally says that an old oak tree had been there since the making of the world. Encompassing the city were olive

trees, grapes, springs, and wells, and touching ground.

The surrender of Machpelah, later purchased by Abraham for a tomb for Sarah, was extremely close. It turned into the internment put of Sarah, as well as of Abraham, Isaac, Jacob, Rebekah, and Leah.

CHAPTER

FOURTEEN

Abram, Lot, Melchizedek
(14:1-24)

Rather than living in peace, thriving, and bliss, part and Abram wound up amidst a war. Effective warring armed forces from the east attacked the place that is known for Palestine, and created much ruin. Abram turned out to be profoundly included on account of his adoration for Lot, and soon uncovered himself as a warrior to be figured with when trespassers looked for loot.

Parcel turned into a wartime captive when his city, Sodom, and the neighboring kingdoms were vanquished by the intruders. He had welcomed inconvenience by making the most of Sodom's straightforwardness and benefit, and by getting to be noticeably one of the general population of that fiendish city.

Presently he found that he needed to share the city's threat and catastrophe. Abram immediately reacted with his 318 men to impact a save, and set up himself as a capable power for exemplary nature in the land.

1. "Amraphel," the "ruler of Shinar." One of the group of four forming the attacking

armed force. "Shinar," situated in northern Mesopotamia, gave its name to the whole zone between the Tigris and Euphrates, including Babylonia. Lower Mesopotamia was the focal point of Sumerian human progress, going back to around 3500 B.C. "Amraphel" was the lord of that area.

Until as of late researchers recognized him with Hammurabi, one of the prior lords of Babylon. In any case, late finds among dirt tablets have tended to set Hammurabi's date closer 1700 B.C. Amraphel was top dog significantly before.

"Arioch" was ruler of "Ellasar," Babylonian Larsa, and most likely controlled a substantially bigger locale in the southern piece of Babylonia.

"Chedorlaomer." King of Elam, a notable mountain district close to the leader of the Persian Gulf. He was by all accounts the most capable of the four lords who made up this undertaking. He had set up control over alternate rulers of Babylonia and Palestine. His name Kudur-Lagamer signifies "hireling of Lagamer," one of Elam's divine beings.

The capital of "Elam" was Susa. "Tidal," the other confederate ruler, was known as the lord of Gotim, i.e., "countries," or people groups. His title may show that he was responsible for a few individual kingdoms, or that he was at the leader of a solid band of wandering individuals who were in the matter of making assaults for loot.

2. These kings, with their select troops, originated from the locale past Damascus, and swooped downward on the nation east of the Jordan to the extent the south end of the Sea of Salt. At that point they turned northward and moved quickly up the western side of the Jordan. The unequivocal fight was foought in the low nation beneath the Dead Sea (the "vale of Siddim," v.3), with the five lords of that prompt area who had defied their eastern overlords.

3. "The salt sea" (Dead Sea) is forty-six miles in length and nine and one-half miles wide. Since the surface of the water is 1,292 feet underneath the level of the Mediterranean, and the water is 1,200 feet profound, this ocean is the "most minimal sheet of water on the planet." Its water is five times more grounded in saline substance than the remnants of Sodom

and Gomorrah lie underneath the waters of the south end of this ocean.

Admah and Zeboiim (cf. v.2) were alternate urban areas pulverized by the ruinous impact from God's hand. The lords of the east brought conclusive thrashing upon the collected warriors and brought detainees and loot with them as they returned. Part was among the caught ones.

6. "And the Horites in their Mount Seir." Archeology has contributed much to build up the fundamental trustworthiness of these early accounts. These individuals, called "Horites," are presently outstanding as Hurrians, a non-Semitic gathering. Their records, revealed at Nuzu by archeologists, have tossed much light on male centric traditions. William F. Albright trusted that these Hurrians became a force to be reckoned with as ahead of schedule as 2400 B.C., and moved toward becoming contenders of Hittites and Sumerians for the matchless quality in culture and learning.

They probably discovered their way to the district south of the Dead Sea very early. They were uprooted from the locale of Mount Seir by Esau's relatives (Deut. 2:22).

7. "Kadesh" (asylum). An antiquated spot where water streamed from a stone, and judgment issued from a heavenly man who got divine disclosure. It was on the fringe of Edom, around fifty miles south of Beer-sheba, and seventy miless from Hebron. Here the Israelites spent an era sitting tight for God's summon to push ahead into Palestine.

Miriam was covered at Kadesh, an eleven-day travel from Sinai, "Amalekites." Rough, savage raiders who wandered the wild region of Palestine. They demonstrated a consistent danger to the Israelites all the times of the kingdom. In this example the general population of Canaan were seriously beaten by the eastern intruders.

10. "Bitumen pits" (AV, sludge pits). Pits from which fluid oil had been expelled. The gaps may in any case have been halfway loaded with the percolating fluid. The battling men, attempting frantically to get away from the rage of the adversary assault, fell into these openings and were decimated. It was a hour of calamity for them. The eastern intruders got away with much loot and numerous prisoners, who might turn into their slaves.

13. "Abram the Hebrew." Quickly the news of the fight achieved Abram at Hebron. He had not been associated with the battling, but rather since his nephew was a detainee, he was doubly committed to endeavor a safeguard. This is the principal use in the Scriptures of "Hebrew" (ha ibri). The correct induction of the name is still in debate.

It was utilized by outsiders in assigning relatives of Abraham and the patriarchs. It most likely signifies "a relative of Eber," or "one from the opposite side" (of the stream). This applies to Abram as one who had moved from Mesopotamia. Some have recognized the "Jews" with the "Habiru," who became a force to be reckoned with in antiquarianism through the Tell el Amarna letters found in Egypt and the Mesopotamian tablets of Nuzu and Mari. The character of these troublesome pirates would not have charmed them to the offspring of Abram.

14. Hebrew riq (AV, "outfitted") portrays the quick, exhaustive work done by Abram in getting each accessible man enthusiastically without a moment's delay. It is interpreted, truly, drew out, as a sword from its casing.

Not a man was cleared out. Three hundred and eighteen men addressed the call to take after their regarded pioneer.

For a foundation, for example, the patriarch kept up, it was important to have s solid power to depend on. Other than these reliable, prepared men, Abram brought with him troops from the agreeable confederates, "Aner," "Eshcol," and "Mamre," who were faithful to their great companion in the hour of crisis.

The escaping trespassers from the east advanced rapidly to Dan at the northern limit of Canaan. The city settled at the foot of Mount Hermon, some separation northwest of Caesarea Philippi. At that Laish (cf. Jud. 18:7). The Danites took it years after the fact and called it "Dan."

15. "Hobah" was a city under fifty miles north of the old city at Damascus. After the assault started at Dan, Abram and his battling men shrouded one hundred miles in the quest for the armed force of Chedorlaomer. In the unexpected assault, recouping all the goods and the detainees.

Part was sheltered again in the keeping of his uncle. What's more, Abram had set up his energy in Canaan, for encompassing people groups would remain in amazement of one who could convey such crushing blows.

17. Coming back to his own particular locale, Abram was met by the lord of Sodom, who communicated genuine a debt of gratitude is in order for the prominent deliverance. They met at a place called Shaveh, or "the lords' dale (AV). The word shaveh signifies "a plain." It was likely close Jerusalem.

18-20. "Melchizedek, king of Salem." The name of this baffling individual means either "lord of uprightness," or, "my ruler is honesty," or "my ruler is Zedek." Zedek is the Hebrew word for "exemplary nature," and furthermore the name of a Canaanite god. Melchizedek was the minister lord of "Salem," which is an abbreviated frame for Urusalim, "city of peace," related to Jerusalem.

The Tell el Amarna tablets recognize "Salem: with Jerusalem as right on time as 1400 B.C. Shalom is the Hebrew word for "peace," and Shalem most likely was the Canaanite divine force of peace.

This, compassionate minister ruler, perceiving Abram's honorability and worth, provided refreshment and sustenance for the tired warrior and his men. These blessings were tokens of fellowship and cordiality. Melchizedek lauded El Elyon, his God (AV, the most high God) for allowing Abram the ability to accomplish triumph. Abram perceived Mellchizedek's 'El Elyon as Jehovah, the God he himself served.

The name "God most high" was found in the Ras Shamra records that go back to the fourteenth century B.C. Obviously Melchizedek had a firm grasp on the tenets of his confidence, which were as valid and fundamental as those brought from Babylonia by Abram.

Each of these stalwarts had a remark and a comment. (See Ps. 110:4; Heb. 5:9,10; 7:1-7) for the advancement of the idea of the perfect ministry and the use of this in the Messianic teaching). The creator of Hebrews proclaims that Christ was of a holy request considerably more old than that of Aaron, and hence his ministry was better than the Aaronic organization. In promote acknowledgment of Melchizedek's consecrated standing, Abram brought tithes as a religious advertising.

21-24. In managing the "king of Sodom," the patriarch declined to acknowledge for himself the body picked up in the fight. He had battled not to advance himself, but rather to secure the arrival of Lot. He would not benefit in any way, but rather would see to ti that his partners had a sensible add up to administer to their costs. Clearly there was not all that much, childish, or getting a handle on in his character.

CHAPTER
FIFTEEN

Abram Promised An Heir
(15:1-21)

For the duration of his life Abram showed a solid confidence in God. It was anything but difficult to give this put stock in a chance to sparkle forward in hours of triumph. When he recollect God's wondrous guarantees to him, he took comfort from the affirmation that their satisfaction was to be in and through his seed.

In any case, when he developed old and saw that the finish of his days was close and that he was as yet childless, he was enticed to be demoralized. His confidence in the guarantees faltered. How could God now satisfy his guarantees? At the point when might he satisfy them? Abram required confirmation. Thus God addressed him.

1. "Fear not... I am thy shield, and thy exceeding great reward." First, Abram must secure dread by confiding in completely in the Lord. This figure of God as a shield was ascertained to give expectation, boldness, and confidence. In any case, safeguard was insufficient. Abram needed before his eyes the

conviction of a reward that would bring the fullest delights.

Maybe the rendering, thy remunerate is to surpass incredible, is closer the importance got from the content in its specific circumstance. The two methods for deciphering these words abandon us confounded until the point that we see that whichever way ensures triumph ahead.

2-7. The Lord guaranteed Abram that he was not to look to "Elizer of Damascus" as his beneficiary, however that his very own genuine child siring would be destined to convey a rich satisfaction to each forecast. In snapshots of risk or misery Abram was to have faith in God's assurance, God's satisfaction of his guarantees, and the boundless number of his relatives.

It was a test to glorious trust. What's more, Abram could accept in light of the fact that he knew the One who had made the guarantees. He realized that Jehovah could be trusted. Despite the fact that no kid was in the home, God would yet fill the earth with the individuals who might think back to Abram as father. Trustful surrender to the will of God is the essential component in genuine religion.

6. "He checked it to him for uprightness." The nature of being appropriate with God is indefinably valuable in the Lord's eyes. Abram was legitimized, i.e., checked upright, on the premise of his faith.

8-21. Instantly Jehovah was prepared to approve the agreement with the man who had yielded himself to the awesome will (cf. Gen. 12:1-3). Hebrew b'rit is differently deciphered "pledge," "reduced," "grave understanding," "confirmation," "settlement." No one of these words brings over into English the full importance of this serious exchange.

In these old circumstances men here and there confirmed an understanding or agreement by going between the parts of a split, conciliatory creature. This "cutting of the pledge" was not in itself a give up. Or maybe, it was a consecrated function by which the men pronounced their serious reason to keep the assention.

Some Bible understudies have brought up that in the occasion recorded in Gen. 15:8-21, just a single emblematic illustrative of the differentiating parties-the "light of flame" (AV marg.), or "blazing light" (cf. Jud. 7:16,20), image of Jehovah-go between the parts of the creatures.

As such, the agreement for this situation was to be kept from God-ward side alone. Just the Lord himself could satisfy its guarantees. He would make Abram's relatives as various as the stars and give them an awesome land, extending from the doors of Egypt to the forceful Euphrates.

CHAPTER
SIXTEEN

Ishmael
(16:1-16)

1-3. "Now Sarai....bear him no children." Abram and Sarai had been married for a long time. No kids had come to light up the home and to satisfy the great predictions. However Jehovah had been particular in his guarantee of a beneficiary (cf. 15:4). As the years moved by, the error between the guarantee and the conditions turned out to be increasingly perplexing.

To be childless was a cataclysm and a disfavor for any Hebrew spouse, and it was much more awful for Sarai. Both a couple more likely than not looked for intends to enable God to work out the satisfaction of his guarantee. They knew the immediate educating of Gen. 2:24, and understood that married couples must adjust to that elevated requirement.

For a man to take an optional spouse or mistress was evil. However, in endeavoring to give an approach to God to do his forecast, Sarai was ready to ignore the heavenly standard and give her female slave, Hagar, to Abram, with the expectation that she may bear a child to the family.

"That I might be builded (Heb. bana, "worked") by her" (AV marg.), she said. whenever men and ladies enable their confidence to separate, they depend on human invention. The Egyptian slave was conveyed to Abram's tent that the family may be "fabricated." But conflict and grief took after as awful results.

4-6a. "And he went in unto Hagar." Sarai was acting in careful accord with the traditions of other individuals in her day (cf. the Nuzu tablets). However, Abram and Sarai were relied upon to hold themselves to a higher standard than that of the general population around them.

Abram, the companion of God, practiced a wealthier confidence and was bound by a purer code. All things considered, be taken after his significant other's recommendation and too Hagar into his tent. Before long the slave started to scorn her fancy woman. What's more, Sarai moved toward becoming upset against her cleaning specialist.

Each of the three of the people in the triangle endured. Sarai pointed the finger at Abram for the entire inconvenience, however he had just completed her recommendation. Desire changed the environment totally, Peace, amicability, and bliss couldn't exist in that home. What's more, the house was on the purpose of separating.

6b. "Dealt hardly with her." Afflicted her. Hebrew 'ana intends to "abuse, discourage, harrow." For this situation it might intend to "aggrieve or abuse." Sarai may have oppressed Hagar with substantial obligations or real discipline. Whatever the mistreatment, it so infuriated, disgraced, or humiliated her as to drive her from her special lady nearness.

Energetic desire and intensity set the two ladies against each other. Furthermore, Abram was very little help to both of them. Conditions deteriorated by the occasion.

7,8. "And the angel of Jehovah found her." In urgency Hagar fled toward her country, Egypt. She was still legitimately a slave and had no privilege to flee. Her circumstance, be that as it may, had turned out to be horrendous, and flight appeared to display the main help. She presumably figured she may discover peace, rest, and life in her old home nation.

When she achieved "Shur" (the divider), she stopped before intersection the outskirt. Here the Egyptians kept up a divider or solid line of fortresses to shield Egypt from intruders from the east. It is said in Egyptian records as right on time as 2000 B.C.

In the calm of the wild Hagar was gone up against by "the heavenly attendant of Jehovah," who had come to bring her heading, expectation, and genuine feelings of serenity. This appearance is the main recorded visit of "the blessed messenger of Jehovah" to earth. It was a snapshot of abnormal noteworthiness. This "blessed messenger" was not a made being, but rather Jehovah himself, showing himself to Hagar.

For different employments of this name, see Gen. 32:30' Exod. 23:20-23; 32:34; I Kings 19:5,7; Isa. 63:9. From these sections it is apparent that the "heavenly attendant" is Jehovah himself, introduce in time and place. He recognizes himself with Jehovah; he talks and acts with God's power; he is discussed as God, or as Jehovah.

9-12. The "angel's" encouraging word to Hagar was that she ought to backpedal to the difficult circumstance she had left, take up her weight, sit tight for the satisfaction of the awesome arrangement, and search for the day when her child, "Ishmael," ought to end up plainly the leader of an essential tribe.

"Ishmael" (God heareth) was to be a "wild ass of a man," with quality and brave and a savage mien.

He would live wild and unshackled, in the wild, without companions or loyalties. His relatives were bound to develop into a compelling swarm of Bedouins, wild, free, slippery, foolhardy men, meandering the open spaces of the abandon.

13-16. "Thou art a God that seeth." Hagar was thrilled to perceive God in the experience, and to see him to be a benevolent, compassionate, astute onlooker of a poor individual in desperate need. She reacted with respectful confidence. The well or spring was named "Brew lahai-return on initial capital investment."

This name had been differently interpreted and revised. Maybe as great a rendering as any is The well of the living one who seeth me. Hagar was moved forcefully by the acknowledgment that she had been in the very nearness of the compelling God and that she was as yet alive. Maybe the well was in the region of Kadesh (cf. 16:14), around fifty miles south of Beersheba. The kid was conceived, and the name Ishmael was given to him by Abram, at that point eighty-six years of age.

CHAPTER

SEVENTEEN

New Promises, And Abraham's Response (17:1-27)

1. "I am the Almighty God (El Shad-day). After thirteen years God appeared to Abram with a consolation, a test, and a wealthier guarantee. He changed Abram's name and that of his better half. He gave particular headings concerning the ritual of circumcision. The awesome name 'El Shadday, with its message that, "Nothing is unimaginable with God, who is almighty and all-adequate," probably conveyed surprising support to Abram.

"El Shadday obviously points out both of these qualities of God. Early Jewish researchers asserted that it was gotten from sh-da, signifying, "He who is adequate." Some researchers get it from the root shadad, "to annihilate." Others relate it to the Assyrian word shadu, "mountain." The LXX gives us hikanos, "adequate." Perhaps the interpreter should remain as close to the significance of "all-capable" as could be expected under the circumstances, particularly since "El talks about power. The One who has all power additionally has all assets to supply each need of his kin.

"Walk before me, and be thou perfect (AV). Such a God could influence such to requests. "Strolling with God" is portrayed in the account concerning Enoch. Presently Abram was instructed to make his day by day life (contemplations, words, deeds) before God completely satisfying to the omniscient eye. Hebrew tamin, "idealize," conveys the feeling of "chaste," or "spotless." But it goes past that sense in recommending a balanced entire, each region rounded out to the full.

3-8. Submissively and respectfully Abram tumbled to the ground to venerate. God's understanding had conveyed the patriarch to the correct demeanor of heart which would make if workable for him to have his name changed, the pledge restored, and the guarantees rehashed. "Abram," has name from birth, is normally characterized as magnified father.

The name "Abraham" has no Hebrew importance, yet the new pledge related with the new name stresses the patriarch's overall mission as God's illustrative to the people groups of the earth (cf. Rom. 4:16,17). Higher benefits were to bring heavier duties. God guaranteed to give unique direction for each progression of the new excursion of confidence and compliance.

9-14. "Circumcised." As an image or token of the pledge, Abraham and his relatives were to receive the custom of circumcision and precisely comply with the directions concerning it. In this way they would give neighboring people groups a ceaseless rest of their devotion and full sense of duty regarding Jehovah.

Circumcision was not another custom. Nor was it bound to the Hebrew individuals. it was generally rehearsed in many parts of the world, particularly in Egypt and Canaan. Assyrians and Babylonians, be that as it may, declined to have any part in it. Not that David hatefully alludes to Goliath as an "uncircumcised Philistine" (I Sam. 17:26; cf. 14:6).

God ordered Abraham to seal the contract between them with the image or token of circumcision. In this manner it would perpetually be the "outward and obvious indication of an internal and undetectable relationship." Every male offspring of Abraham's family unit was to encounter this supernaturally summoned ritual on his eighth day.

15,16. "Sarah." The name Sarai had been borne by Abraham's significant other for a long time. Presently God directed that her name be changed to "Sarah," Princess. It is the ladylike type of sar, "ruler." This new name underscored the part Abraham's better half was to play later on, as mother of countries. Abraham is looked upon as "Father Abraham" by Jews, Mohammedans, and Christians. It is well to recollect that Sarah, as well, have a key impact in the dramatization of the ages.

17-22. Once more "Abraham fell upon the face" before the Lord. God had anticipated that the hotly anticipated child would without a doubt be destined to his significant other. In spite of the fact that Sarah was ninety years old, she was yet to have the delight of respecting a child through whom God's pledge guarantees would be satisfied.

Abraham had come to look upon Ishmael as his beneficiary and to trust that the brilliant guarantees must be satisfied through him (cf. v.18). Presently he confronted the beyond any doubt word that "Isaac" would be destined to be the offspring of guarantee. "Abraham... laughed" (v.17). He was overpowered. There is no recommendation here of unbelief but instead proof of ponder and extraordinary joy. Abraham was scarcely to fathom such a bewildering declaration. Hebrew sha-haq signifies "to snicker." It is the root verb from which "Isaac" is inferred. Think about Sarah's response and her giggling in 18:12. There was a chosen contrast in the reasons for giggling in the two occasions.

23-27. Abraham was moved by confidence and loyal soul to complete the summon of God. Promptly he established the ceremony of circumcision all through his organization. Ishmael was among those circumcised. Abraham was obeying God and making himself and his family qualified to satisfy the celestial purposes. The Lord's intends to reach and favor every one of the countries was advancing toward satisfaction.

CHAPTER

EIGHTEEN

Sodom And Gomorrah
(18:1-19:38)

1. "The terebinths (AV, plains) of Mamre." The living arrangement of Abraham was in the prompt region of Hebron. In spite of the fact that the Hebrew word 'elon can be interpreted "oak" or "terebinth," the last is most likely to be favored. These trees were hallowed trees of the Canaanite asylum of Hebron. The give in of Machpelah was situated in a similar place. The patriarch was in close touch with the sacrosanct places and holy spots. As the centuries progressed, old oaks or terebinth have been recognized as going back to male centric circumstances. "Jehovah appeared."

Despite the fact that Abraham did not immediately perceive the divine guest as the Lord, it soon turned out to be clear to him that the main guest of the three envoys was Jehovah himself. He was "the blessed messenger of Jehovah,: who seems a few times in the prior pages of Genesis.

2-5. "He ran to meet them....and bowed himself toward the ground." Abraham demonstrated uncommonly friendly. He did everything for his visitors that Oriental cordiality could recommend. His way was all that could be inquired. He made prepared to give these glorious guests a regal welcome. He welcomed them to "rest" (AV) or lean back and "comfort" themselves while the dinner was being readied. Hebrew sa advertisement, "comfort" intends to fortify or "make solid." Both the rest and sustenance would give "comfort."

6-8. "Make ready quickly three measures of fine meal." Abraham and Sarah and Ishmael (the fellow) went rapidly about the undertaking of reviving the visitors. A "measure," se a, was on third of an ephah, or about a peck and a half. Two Hebrew words, gem'ah and solet, are utilized to assign the excellent character of the flour utilized as a part of making the moves for the dinner. Hem'a "coagulated drain" blended with crisp drain, was an invigorating beverage served to tired travellllers while the more generous sustenance was being readied. The "calf" was an uncommon and included extravagance accommodated these recognized guests.

9-15. The Lord plainly and unmistakably pronounced that a kid would be destined to Sarah when the season wakes up once more

(AV, "As indicated by the season of life). The glad occasion was just a year away. God had not overlooked his guarantee but rather was moving in the direction of its extraordinary satisfaction. "Was tuning in" (AV, heard). The Hebrew shoma'at shows tuning in right then and there.

"Progressed in years" (AV, will stricken in age). From the Hebrew figure of speech signifying "went into days." "Sarah giggled." Sarah chuckled in sheer wariness as she however how incomprehensible it was for her to endure a kid. She here portrays herself as b'loti, "exhausted," "shriveled," "prepared to go to pieces, as an article of clothing." She recollected that Abraham, as well, was old and past the period of parenthood.

The heavenly word guaranteed Sarah and Abraham that nothing is "too hard" (lit., awesome) "for the Lord." Even if the thing is to be done was uncommon, exceptional, or past common conduct, Jehovah was equipped for achieving it whenever and in any capacity he picked. "For with God nothing should be incomprehensible" (Lk. 1:37). In the introduction of Isaac, as in the introduction of Jesus, it was vital for God to work a marvel.

16-22. Sodom....Gomorrah. The two driving urban communities at the south end of the Dead Sea. The others – Admah, Zeboliim, and Zoar – were to be pulverized alongside Sodom and Gomorrah in the blaze that was to cleanse the cesspools of wrongdoing. (Eventually God saved Zoar as another home for Lot.) The Scripture plainly demonstrates that a perfect appearance was to bring ghastly judgment and fate upon the corrupt tenants. The urban areas were around eighteen miles from Abraham's home at Hebron, It was workable for him to see the southern end of the Sea from the prompt region of Hebron.

22-33. In his great petition of intervention for the couple of equitable men in Sodom, Abraham uncovered the wealthier components of his character-his liberality, sensitivity, his anxiety for honesty in God and man. He demonstrated that he comprehended God's eagerness to excuse and give full absolve, and to manage His animals, however underhanded, as per uncovered benchmarks of equity and honesty.

He realized that Jehovah could be relied on to act with regards to is sacred nature.

At the point when Abraham left off mediating, he had God's guarantee that He would save Sodom if upwards of ten honest people could be discovered in that. be that as it may, when the required number couldn't be discovered, nothing could deflect the disaster. Intercessory petition dependably draws out the best in men. Their unselfish worry for others sparkles like a delightful gem. In begging the Lord, Abraham obviously showed veritable love and concern. What's more, he encountered once again the companionship of God in His eagerness to guide with him and give him an extraordinary disclosure before the fate fell.

CHAPTER

NINETEEN

Lot Sat In The Gate Of Sodom
(19:1-38)

Lot had accomplished some unmistakable quality among his kindred natives in the mischievous city. Maybe his sitting in the door demonstrates that he helped dispense equity to the general population. Be that as it may, to the magnificent guests, powerless, common, narrow minded Lot more likely than not been a terrible figure. He quickly volunteered to fill the role of a rich host to the two outsiders.

4-22. The unfortunate involvement with the men of the city, at Lots house, showed that the ugliest circumstance possible won in Sodom. the heavenly attendants, who had gone under awesome requests to find the degree of human wickedness there, required no further revelation. The most wretched, most unspeakable brand of transgression was polished transparently and boldly.

The flag-bearers (angels) from God had just to articulate authority sentence, give due notice, and find all around conceivable to lead Lot and his hesitant family from the destined city. Flurry was fundamental. Inadequate dutifulness was requested. Part looked for wildly to caution and convince those of his own family to clear out. Be that as it may, as the account lets us know, "he appeared unto his children in-law as one who taunted" (joked, ASV).

Parcel had acted egotistically and absurdly when he had turned into a piece of Sodom, where his youngsters would be grimy by the city's disgrace. In spite of the fact that he had achieved some measure of noticeable quality among the general population, he had never affected them toward honorable conduct; thus he neglected to apply moral authority in the hour of emergency.

His own particular family, toward the end, put no confidence in his most dire notices. What a striking complexity between the wickedness of Lot and the noble existence of Abraham! The individuals from Lot's family were all degenerate. Not one of them measured an ounce in the balances of equity and exemplary nature. Whenever Lot and his significant other and two girls bumbled out of the bound city, God kept down the looming demolition until the point when his errand people could remove them from the detestable grasp of Sodom.

23-25. "Jehovah rained.....brimstone and fire." It is well to consider truly, as recording an unmistakable judgment of the Lord upon individuals so degenerate that they had no privilege to live.

It was inside God's energy to deliver a seismic tremor that would open a gap in the stones to discharge stockpiled gas that would detonate and toss monstrous supplies of oil into the air.

At the point when all the inflammable stuff was touched off, sheets of exacting flame poured back to finish the devastation. Singing blazes and dark smoke more likely than not secured each territory of the city, covering and devouring each living thing.

26. "A pillar of salt." Lot's significant other (wife) endeavored to get away from the approaching catastrophe. However, she let her interest and her unnecessary love for the things of Sodom (and also for her family, likely) make her resist requests and think back. It was a deadly demonstration. The lady was settled to the spot, and her body turned into a "mainstay of salt," secured and encrusted with stores from the down-pouring brimstone.

There it remained for a long time, a loathsome cautioning against insubordination to the particular charge of God, and a quiet indication of the Lord's constant character. Somebody has stated: "She stood, a noiseless sentinel to corrupt narrow-mindedness."

Indeed, even right up 'til the present time columns and apexes of salt are unmistakable in the zone south to help his devotees to remember the unfortunate outcomes of adoring unimportant things, forewarned them to "recollect Lot's significant other" (Lk. 17:32).

27,28. "The smoke of the land went up as the smoke of a furnace." Abraham remained on the statures close Hebron and looked upon the inferno in the valley beneath. He had done everything he could to save Lot and his family. Presently he viewed the devastation of the four pagan urban areas that had been so impolite in their conduct. Clearly the wages of transgression is demise.

30-38. "Two daughters." The end section in the vocation of Lot is a forlorn one. It portrays perverted relations that we would like to overlook. The two little girls, raised in underhanded Sodom, stooped sufficiently low to take part in a demonstration that is unspeakably loathsome. The consequence of that deed was the introduction of two young men, who turned into the forebears of the Moabites and Ammonites.

Lot and his family bombed hopelessly. Calamity. disfavor. gloom, and passing are composed in their commemoration. "Be not beguiled; God is not ridiculed; for at all a man soweth, that should he likewise procure" (Gal.6:7).

CHAPTER
TWENTY

Abraham And Abimelech
(20:1-18)

The unfortunate scene adds another woeful line to the photo of the patriarch. For what reason did he commit a similar error twice? (cf. 12:11-20) Why should God's decision agent fail so as to give an agnostic lord open door for a merited censure? Through dread and transitory shiftiness, Abraham turned to deception, misdirection, and by and large distortion.

1. "Abraham....sojourned to Gerar." "Gerar" was most likely five or six miles south of Gaza, and in this way a piece of the region having a place with the Philistines. A few analysts, in any case, have found it around thirteen miles southwest of Kadesh.

4-6. "Integrity of my heart....innocency of my hands." Abimelech, who governed over the general population of Gerar, was uncommonly legit, moral, and reasonable. His cases to "integrity," i.e., "immaculateness" or "earnestness" and "innocency" set him out as a man of elevated expectations. At the point when cautioned in a fantasy by Jehovah, he met the trouble soundly and manfully. He showed up in a superior light than God's illustrative.

7. Here Abraham is known as a connection to the Lord. He approached God, was secured by divine power, got uncommon disclosure, and was committed to represent God the message he had gotten.

9-16. Abimelech censured Abraham, reestablished Sarah to him, and, what's more, offered to him sheep, bulls, and slaves, and a unique fortune (maybe equivalent to almost four hundred dollars); and he guaranteed Abraham of a home in his kingdom.

17,18. Consequently, Abraham petitioned God for the ruler that the suffering God had sent upon him and his kin may be evacuated. The patriarch withdrew from Abimelech a more astute, if a sadder, man. He was discovering that Jehovah's hand had arrived to satisfy his destiny.

CHAPTER

TWENTY-ONE

Isaac Born; Ishmael Driven Away (21:1-21)

1-7. "Visited." From paqad, "to visit," in the feeling of "bringing a judgment or a gift." For this situation it was a cherished gift God brought. Divine beauty and power created the wonder. "Sarah....bare Abraham a child in his seniority." True to his guarantee, God gave a kid to Sarah and Abraham. Each pledge forecast was to have divine satisfaction through this child of Abraham.

The father had the delight of naming the chap, and afterward the benefit of circumcising him when he was eight days old. At the point when Sarah held the angel in her arms, her euphoria knew no limits. For a long time she had lived for that consecrated minute. She stated: "God hath made me to snicker (ASV, arranged giggling for me); everybody that heareth will chuckle with me."

For the neighbors, it would be the giggling of amiable shock combined with veritable enjoyment and generous felicitation. For Sarah, it was the happy chuckling of wondrous acknowledgment. She held in her arms God's blessing to the world. It was a remarkable snapshot of thanksgiving, delight, and consecrated devotion.

8. "And the child grew." The day for weaning youthful Isaac, likely when he was three years of age, was a major occasion in the life of all the family. It was an event to be praised with cheering and devouring.

9-11. Before long, nonetheless, inconvenience emerged. "Sarah saw the child of Hagar.... mocking. Sarah had beforehand endured as a result of Hagar and Ishmael. Presently the contention was restored when Sarah saw Hagar's child associated with conduct that angered her. The Hebrew word m'saheq is an escalated (piel) type of the verb on which the word Isaac is fabricated. It has been interpreted "deriding," "donning," "playing," and "making sport." There is no justifiable reason here to present "ridiculing."

What Ishmael was doing does but rather make a difference the way that it enraged Sarah. Maybe she essentially couldn't stand to see her child playing with Ishmael as with an equivalent. Or, then again it might be that envy took full control. Sarah may have expected that

Abraham, out of affection for Ishmael, would give the more seasoned fellow the conspicuous place in the legacy.

At any rate, the family life couldn't go ahead as it seemed to be. Hagar and Ishmael needed to go. To drive them out more likely than not been exceedingly "intolerable" to Abraham was to release Hagar and Ishmael, as Sarah requested. So as to come, Ishmael would be the father of an extraordinary country. In any case, Isaac was to be beneficiary of the guarantees and convey gift to all the world – "in Isaac might thy seed be called."

Reluctantly, Abraham sent Hagar and Ishmael away toward the wild, conveying a goatskin bottle loaded with crisp water. It is not clear how old Ishmael was. Cautious investigation of the Hebrew content leaves the understudy allowed to consider him a youthful pre-adult, maybe around sixteen years old.

14c-16. "Beer-sheba," on the fringe of Egypt, was around fifty miles south of Jerusalem and twenty-seven miles south of Hebron. For those going southward, it was the last purpose of any noteworthiness in Palestine. In that dry wild territory, these two explorers couldn't would like to exist numerous hours without encountering extraordinary thirst.

At the point when the water gave out, weariness grabbed hold of the kid; and his mom laid him down in the little shade of a bush to pass on. In any case, God, in his kindness and love, mediated to bring expectation, life, and confirmation.

17-19. "God heard the voice of the lad." The Lord gave a lot of crisp, streaming water, and saved the life of the kid. For both mother and child another day had unfolded.

20,21. "And God was with the lad." It was obvious that God expected to satisfy his guarantee in regards to this child of Abraham; he would make him the colossal country of Ishmaelites.

Abimelech And Abraham
(21:22-34)

At the point when inconvenience emerged (v.25) between the men of Abraham and those of Abimelech, the two bosses consented to go into a pledge with each other. Initially, they fixed challenges and redressed shameful acts.

At that point Abraham offered blessings to the ruler to endorse the arrangement.

Notwithstanding different things, he exhibited seven ewe sheep to Abimelech. "Along these lines they made an agreement at Beer-shea (v. 32).

The comparability of the Hebrew words sheba', "seven," and shaba', "swear," appears to demonstrated that there is an association between them.

In like manner, "Lager sheba" may signify "well of seven" or "well of swearing." The reflexive utilization of the word for "to swear" signifies "to seven Oneself" or to promise oneself by seven hallowed things. In full sense of duty regarding the agreement, Abraham offered thanks to the "everlasting God" ('Elohim, v.33).

The patriarch would soon walk off the mmap of history, yet his God, the unchangeable, Eternal One would remain. Clearly Abraham had established a permanent connection on the agnostic ruler, Abimelech, for in his own specific manner, the lord recognized his loyalty to the God of Abraham.

CHAPTER
TWENTY-TWO

Abraham And Issac
(22:1-19)

Abraham's preeminent trial of confidence and compliance came after Ishmael been sent away, when all expectations for what's to come were held up in Isaac.

1. "God did proved Abraham." Hebrew nissa, "demonstrate") AV, entice), connotes a testing that would uncover Abraham's confidence as nothing else had done. He should give proof of total submission and unquestioning trust in Jehovah, should even obey indiscriminately, continuing well ordered until the point that the confidence emerged as plainly as the afternoon sun.

Abraham went through the fiercest flames, stood up under the mightiest weight, and persevered through the most troublesome strain, to rise up out of the trial in entire triumph.

2. No test could have been more serious than the one God now forced. What's more, no dutifulness could have been more immaculate than Abraham's. At the point when God called, the patriarch reacted speedily. Notwithstanding when he realized what was ahead, he placidly

addressed his hirelings: "Tolerate ye here....I and the chap will go there and love, and return again to you" (v.5).

His confidence in the God who sees and "makes sure" guaranteed him that all eventual well. He confided in Jehovah to do his guarantees. "By confidence Abraham, being attempted, presented Isaac: yea, he that had happily gotten the guarantees was putting forth up his lone generated child; even he to whom it was stated, In Isaac might thy seed be called: bookkeeping that God can raise up, even from the dead; from whence he did likewise in a figure get him back" (Heb. 11:17-19). Confidence saw past the relinquish and was eager to comply.

"Moriah." The place of the yield can't be emphatically recognized. II Chronicles 3:1 appears to find it on the site of Solomon's Temple. Convention has held to this view, and it is hard to locate an all the more effectively acknowledged spot. The adventure by walking from Beer-sheba more likely than not taken most of three days.

"Offer him...for a burnt offering." The Hebrew word utilized here, 'ala, actually, lift him up, means the offering of the casualty in general consumed offing in total commitment. No reference is made to killing the kid. The first expectation of Jehovah, obviously, was to ensure the total offering, yet to meddle before the casualty was killed.

God's motivation, to a limited extent, was to display a question lesson portraying his loathing of human give up as it was straightforwardly polished by the barbarian on all sides.

7,8. As the two walked along up the side of the mountain, the perceptive youth asked: "Where is the lamb for a consumed offering?" How regrettable! The appropriate response of the father came immediately: "God will give himself a sheep to a consumed offering." The verb signifies "to see."

In reality, Abraham was stating that Jehovah could see to that in his own particular manner. He had inside his heart a calm affirmation that God could look after such points of interest. Abraham did not realize that the kid would be saved the experience of death, yet he had the confidence to trust that the supreme One would give whatever was vital in his own specific manner and time.

Paul went into the profundities of this fact when he stated: "He saved not his own particular Son, but rather conveyed him up for every one of us, in what manner should he not with him likewise uninhibitedly give all of us things" (Rom. 8:32).

9,10. Everything was set up on the sacrificial table. The adored chap of the guarantees was bound and prostrate upon the wood he had expedited his own shoulders. The fire was prepared. Everything was still and calm. The sharp blade was unsheathed and lifted high.

12,13. All of a sudden the voice from paradise broke the stillness. God charged Abraham to drop the blade, free the kid from his thongs, and get the slam from his place the shrubbery. It was Abraham's most astounding hour. God had attempted his heart and was fulfilled. Isaac again remained by his dad's side, an observer of the Lord's benevolence, beauty, and arrangement (cf. v. 14).

It is not odd that Jesus should state: "Your dad Abraham cheered to see my day: and he saw it, and was happy" (Jn. 8:56). The godly man came back to Beer-sheba aglow with the feeling of the nearness of God. He could never be the same again. The considerable guarantees had been reestablished, and he was guaranteed that the contract endowments would happen upon him and his relatives.

CHAPTER
TWENTY-THREE

Sarah's Death And Burial
(23:1-20)

1,2. "Sarah died in….Hebron." At 127 years old Sarah passed away, leaving Abraham bowed in sadness. His affection for her had been real and delicate. She was to him "the princess." We may well envision that amid dim hours and glad ones, she had been a steadying prop for his confidence and a wellspring of quality in all the trip. They had moved from Beersheba to Hebron, a city eighteen miles south of Jerusalem.

Isaac was presently thirty-seven years of age. In his distress Abraham uncovered something of the poise of soul that portrays a solid righteous man. Other than howling and generally uproariously showing his sorrow, he broke forward into sobbing. The Hebrew words for "grieve" and "sob" convey the two thoughts.

3-20. In due time, in any case, "he ascended" (AV, stood up) from his griever's place on the ground and went manfully about the matter of acquiring a covering spot and organizing the memorial service. Rather than taking Sarah's body back to Haran or Ur, he found a tomb in the land God had given him.

He managed the local Hittites and purchased, at impressive cost, "the give in of Machpelah" so his family may claim a decision covering place forever to come. In exchanging with the proprietors, Ephron and the others, he called himself a "sojourner" and a "pilgrim" in that piece of the world, showing that his beginning was remote and his time of remain in the land dubious. The offspring of Heth (Hittites) called him "a powerful ruler" (AV) or a sovereign of God (v.6).

They held him in high regard. Machpelah, a twofold buckle, turned into the internment place of Sarah. Abraham, Isaac, Rebekah, Jacob, and Leah. In later years it turned into a Moslem ownership, and a mosque was worked over it.

CHAPTER
TWENTY-FOUR

Eliezer, Isaac, And Rebekah
(24:1-67)

The old patriarch was very much progressed in years (Heb. gone into days). Isaac was as yet unmarried. Abraham was worried that his beneficiary discover a spouse from his own particular individuals, rather than from the Canaanites. He picked his confided in worker, Eliezar, to make the long adventure to Mesopotamia to discover Isaac's lady of the hour.

1-9. "Abraham said unto his eldest servant.... take a wife unto my son Isaac (AV). Before Eliezer left, Abraham gave him full headings and requested from him a hallowed promise. Putting a hand under another's thigh was a serious method for meaning that if the pledge were disregarded, the kids, yet unborn, would retaliate for the demonstration of traitorousness. By methods for the vow, the worker would be bound all the more viably to secure a satisfactory spouse for Isaac. Abraham guaranteed him of God's assistance: "He should send his holy messenger before thee, and thou shalt take a spouse unto my child from thus (AV).

10-14. "And the servant .... arose, and went.... unto the city of Nahor." The worker had been guaranteed divine direction, and he was on edge to be driven. An ardent man, who tried to know God's will, he asked intensely and honestly that moment headings may be given. A mix-up, he felt, would be deplorable. Without a doubt Eliezer was God's man for a profoundly imperative mission.

"The city of Nahor." Either the city of Haran or a city named Nahor in the region of Haran. "Mesopotamia" is the interpretation of the Hebrew which may actually be rendered "Aram of the two waterways," i.e., the district of the Tigris and Euphratess stream valleys. Bethuel was the father of Laban and Rebekah. His folks were Nahor and Milcah. Abraham was his uncle.

15-28. At the point when the worker met Rrebekah at the well, he was persuaded that God had addressed his petition and had guided him straightforwardly to her. The young lady was excellent and shrewd, and addressed correctly to each prerequisite he had stipulated. So Elliezer gave her a couple of preparatory blessings a ring for the nose and after that two wrist trinkets, all garish and amazingly important. Different blessings were to take after when the family accumulated in the tent of Rebekah's mom.

29-31. "Laban....Eliezer....Rebekah." Laban deceived his actual character when, after observing the costly ring and wrist trinkets, he chose that nothing ought to be saved in clutching Eliezar. He couldn't neglect to be cordial to a man who could influence such to endowments.

The adornments were however the start. Before long gems of silver and gems of gold, and delightful garments were gave to Rebekah. Also, "valuable things (v. 53), extraordinary endowments, were exhibited to the mother and the sibling of the lady of the hour. In a way these blessings compensated for the loss of such a darling individual from the family. The custom of showing profitable endowments to the individuals from the lady's family backpedals in any event to the extent time of Hammurabi (1728-1686 B.C.). Maybe it left the time when the lady was really obtained.

34-48. Eliezar described in some detail the striking satisfaction of his supplication for direction and affirmation. The genuine man realized that the Lord drove him and that Rebekah was God's decision for his young ace.

49-61. Without sitting tight for a meeting with the chose lady, alternate individuals from the family gave their unmistakable responsibility: Rebekah would be Isaac's lady of the hour. They were arranged to keep the young lady for some time (maybe for a while), however the lady, when asked what she favored, proclaimed her readiness to start the excursion promptly.

It was an earth shattering choice for a young lady to make. Her new home was far off, and she would presumably never observe her family again. She was venturing out on confidence, even as Abraham had done a very long time some time recently. New life in Canaan was to be her reward.

62-65. "Isaac went out to meditate." Isaac was sitting tight for his lady of the hour close Beelahai-return for capital invested, where Hagar had discovered expectation and cheer and celestial course. Hebrew suah, generally deciphered "think,: has been rendered "stroll about," "implore," "cry," "regret," or "groan." Verse 67 may toss some light on its significance. Isaac required consoling. It is conceivable that

Sarah had passed away amid the nonappearance of Eliezar. The account depicts Rebekah as actually jumping down from the camel in regard for Isaac and appropriate thought for his significance. She immediately balanced her shroud, with regards to acknowledged principles of behavior. A pledged lady stayed hidden until the point when the marriage had been fulfilled. At exactly that point may her significant other look upon her face.

66,67. Eliezer gave Isaac a full report of all that had occurred on the long adventure. Isaac saw that God had driven the worker to pick Rebekah and perceived that His will in the issue was to be done. He introduced Rebekah in Sarah's own particular tent, and accordingly she turned into the primary woman of the land.

Two verbs remain in the end verse of the section: "Isaac....loved her; and ....was console." Love worked out easily, conveying solace and euphoria to Isaac's heart. It was fitting that the forlorn soul should discover a lady who was dazzling and adorable. Isaac's adoration incited comprehension, chivalrousness, and delicacy of soul. It was particularly great that the young lady, so distant from home, was honored with a spouse who genuinely adore her.

"Comfort" has much more profound hints when considered in the light of heart and home and marriage. Isaac remained in urgent need of "comfort." Rebekah gave something that had been tragically missing since the home-going of his mom. Hebrew naham, "comfort," really intends to give quality or resilience (cf. Jer. 10:4, where the icon manufacturer is said to "comfort his object of worship with nails and with hammers").

The man of peaceful, aloof, bashful confidence was participated in marriage to a lady so intense, so bold, so aggressive, that she was bound to acquire him melancholy the years ahead. However God was driving, and would utilize even blemished people to work out his will for his kin.

CHAPTER

TWENTY-FIVE

Closing Days Of Abraham
(25:1-18)

1-6. "Abraham took a wife....Keturah." In addition to Sarah and Hagar, Abrahan took Keturah as a secondary wife or concubine (I Chr. 1:32). This probably happened numerous years prior to the demise of Sarah, for a few children are recorded. The children and grandsons of Hagar and Keturah got blessings from the hand of Abraham, however all property and expert and profound belonging went to Isaac, the normal lawful beneficiary.

7-10. At 175 years old Abraham arrived at the finish of his natural stay and lapsed. "He surrendered the phantom." The articulation is gotten from Hebrew gawa', "to inhale out his breath," "to come up short," "to sink." Immediately he was" gathered to his dad's family (actually, and relocated to Sheol, the place of left spirits. "He kicked the bucket in a decent old age....and full."

A fitting memorial for an incredible godly man. His life was genuinely completed and completely adjusted. He had lived intrepidly. He had pushed ahead in confidence en route called attention to by God. Remaining by the tomb at the give in of Machpelah were the two children (v.9) whom he had adored with unbeatable love. Isaac and Ishmael were joined in a typical distress and a typical commitment to the person who had implied most to them.

Without a doubt Isaac was reinforced in his deprivation by the acknowledgment that he remained in the uncommon support of God and would not need to bear on alone. For he could be the beneficiary of the rich contract favors guaranteed to and through Abraham.

Isaac And His Family
(25:19-34)

19-23. Sarah, Rebekah, Rachel, and Hannah were all fruitless, and along these lines childless until late in life. It was a deplorable ordeal for each of them. "Issac begged the Lord" for Rebekah. The Hebrew verb 'atar signifies "to ask as a supplant," "to beseech." When it is utilized as a part of the aloof sense, it demonstrates that the subject has honey bee persuaded by methods for imploring, and has replied.

Isaac asked intensely for his fruitless spouse, and Jehovah respected the supplication. Rebekah stopped to be sterile, and imagined. Winning petition had been respected by God.

24-34. "There were twins in her womb" (v.24). Indeed, even before Esau and Jacob were conceived, they battled with each other in their parental imprisonment. What's more, they proceeded with the contention as they grew up. Today their numerous relatives are energetically endeavoring to pick up the preferred standpoint over each other in the Middle East.

Esau turned into the shaggy man of the field, with little energy about otherworldly esteems. He dove boldly along through life, just to get himself cheated of the best things and checkmated by a craftiness supplanter. Jacob got his motivation from Rebekah, who persevered relentlessly to pick up her closures.

Isaac was excessively weak, making it impossible to stay up to date with naughty doings or to manage the blend of Jacob and Rebekah. Esau appeared to be worried about material issues as it were. To him, the inheritance, which included both material and profound endowments, appeared of little an incentive until the point when he had bartered it away.

The claim was the ownership of the principal conceived. It promised him a more fair position than his brother's, the best of the domain, and the wealthiest land, and the pledge gifts God had guaranteed to Abraham and to his relatives. The claim was Esau's since God had enabled him to be conceived first.

Neither Esau nor Jacob demonstrated any estimable enthusiasm for profound fortunes. Every wa shamefully narrow minded and needed comprehension of what conduct would fit a man to be sovereign of God. Jacob was driven to accumulate in for himself everything that would give him the pre-prominence.

Rebekah provided the spaark and the conspiring that secured focal points for her most loved child. He had far to go to end up noticeably the otherworldly pioneer of the individuals who might love Jehovah. Be that as it may, God was understanding; he was not in a rush; he would prepare his pioneer.

Esau made his home in the rough slopes of Edom. A long time later his relatives, the general population of the country he established, would uncover a similar kind of supposing he had appeared and the same degrade ignore for endless program of Jehovah of hosts. Disregarding every demoralizing occurrence, the kingdom of God would advance toward the more full acknowledgment of the heavenly reason.

CHAPTER
TWENTY-SIX

Isaac And Abimelech
(26:1-35)

1. And Isaac went unto Abimelech. Since there was a starvation in Canaan, Isaac went to live briefly in the place where there is the Philistines. This Abimelech, "ruler of the Philistines," was not the Abimelech of Abraham's encounters. The name may have been a dynastic name of the rulers in Philista. "Gerar." A little settlement headed straight toward Egypt, around eleven miles southeast of Gaza.

2-5. Isaac was very nearly choosing to proceed onward to Egypt to look for more ample nourishment and pasturage, when Jehovah appeared to him in a unique theophany. The Lord cautioned Isaac not to go to Egypt, and urged him to stay in Philista until the point that he could go to abide in the pledge arrive. "I will be with thee," he stated, "and will favor thee" (v.3).

Right now Jehovah unquestionably reestablished the guarantees he had made to Abraham. He unmistakably clarified that he was giving those gifts on Isaac in light of his dad's devotion and steadfastness. Abraham had complied with God's voice and kept his charges, instructions, statutes, and laws. Isaac could bring trust and look with confirmation in rehashed achievements of God's guarantees en route. Furthermore, he could rely on having his impact in God's arrangement, officially laid out for seeing to all people groups.

6-11. "She is my sister" (v.7). Isaac uncovered something of his human shortcoming, in Gerar, when he let fear deceive him into lying about his significant other, Rebekah. Similarly as Abraham had done on two events, Isaac looked to pass his significant other off as his sister. At the point when Abimelech watched him enjoying conduct toward Rebekah that was more fitting for a spouse than for a sibling, he reprimanded Isaac pointedly for his duplicity. Once more, one who was outside the contract conveyed a stinging censure to one who ought to have been unquestionably sound.

12-22. Following this despicable scene, Isaac settled down to the sort of prosperous cultivating that made him the envy of all the encompassing neighbors. Indeed, even Abimelech wound up plainly jealous and issued a request that Isaac must leave his domain. The rich property proprietor proceeded onward a short separation to start life once more.

He found that the locals had ceased up the wells that had been water-giving endowments since Abraham's days.

Isaac had his workers revive every one of these wells and furthermore burrow new ones. At whatever point the men burrowed new wells, the Philistines raised much hell for them. The patriarch named his first new well "Esek," conflict, and the second "Sitnah," hostility. The third well, which was done without strife, he called R'hobot, expansive spots.

23-33. Proceeding onward to the region of "Brew sheba," Isaac got a unique correspondence from Jehovah guaranteeing him of abnormal and proceeded with endowments "Dread not, for I.....will favor thee (v.24).

Since he was back again in consecrated an area, it was especially fitting that he assemble a sacrificial stone to Jehovah and accordingly declare to all that he was focused on the undertaking set out for him. Isaac started to give proof of a genuine soul that he had not up to this point uncovered so unmistakably.

CHAPTER
TWENTY-SEVEN

Jacob
(27:1-36:43)

Jacob And Esau
(27:1-46)

It is hard to envision all the feeling, anguish, and savage disillusionment wrapped up in this beautiful account. The old patriarch, with blinded eyes and a tottering edge, now made arrangements to give the holy gift to his first-conceived child. Be that as it may, the cunning Rebekah, who tune in to his headings to Esau, promptly start subverting and disappointing his designs.

Her most loved child, Jacob, as of now had the bequest; she was resolved that he ought to get the oral gift, as well, from the lips of the Lord's illustrative, so all eventual well with the celestial legacy. She couldn't hazard sitting tight for God to work out his designs in his own particular manner. So she turned to the most awful double dealing to secure the gift for her more youthful child.

18-29. "And Jacob said....I am Esau thy firstborn." Coached by his mom, Jacob preceded his old father with duplicity and untruths. He even announced that Jehovah had helped him make his arrangements with speed. In the wake of deceiving his dad, he painted a false kiss upon the old man's upturned face.

30-40. "And Esau lifted up his voice, and wept" (v38). The catastrophe for Esau was that he was totally unmindful of the consecration of the gift, and just wanted the preferences it would give. His profound hurt that Jacob had outsmarted him in securing the inheritance, his astringent disillusionment, his woeful wailing, and the consuming disgrace that immediately ignited into extreme scorn and want for exact retribution are profoundly moving.

41-46. "Arise, flee thou to Laban." To spare Jacob from his sibling's reprisal, Rebekah found an affectation for sending him away. Which of these three-Rebekah, Jacob, or Esau-was most to be felt sorry for? Their family life was wrecked, and each needed to manage forlorn hours of division, thwarted expectation, and lament.

Rebekah could never observe her most loved child again, and Jacob would need to confront existence without father, mother, or sibling.

Furthermore, shouldn't something be said about God's gets ready for the kingdom?

How might they be worked out notwithstanding such childishness, interest, and trickery? The Lord of hosts is not to be defeated by men's restriction, disappointment, or absence of confidence. He can influence his will to win notwithstanding all.

While Isaac drew a little nearer to the hour of his passing, and Rebekah grieved as a result of the upsetting circumstance she had encouraged, and Esau thought of requital, Jacob made his desolate path from Beer-sheba to Padan-aram.

CHAPTER
TWENTY-EIGHT

Jacob, Laban, Leah, And Rachel
(28:1-30:43)

1-5. Isaac blessed him, and charged him.... go to Padan-aram (vv. 1,2). Isaac did not release Jacob away without a gift. He talked in the tone of prophetic articulation, and in wonderful dialect that uncovers his otherworldly recognition. Jacob was to look for a spouse among his relatives in Haran, yet he was to be most worried about going into the rich legacy guaranteed to Abraham.

Isaac approached 'El Shadday, "God Almighty" (v. 3), to give wellbeing, thriving, and sharp comprehension to prepare Jacob for otherworldly initiative. He forecasted that if his child would confer his way to the Lord, the gifts God had guaranteed to Abraham would all be his. Through Isaac, God gave Jacob an order, a test, a confirmation, and heading for the adventure.

6-9. Esau watched and tuned in, at that point went to Ishmael's home to get for himself a spouse of the family line, who might satisfy his folks. Evidently, he needed to attempt the correct way. But since he was essentially common, his vocation in the place where there is Edom missed the mark concerning conduct that could satisfy the Lord Jehovah.

10-17. Jacob made the trip from Beer-sheba to Luz, around twelve miles north of Jerusalem, where he spent the night. Bethel was in that quick region. In the night he was respected with a unique correspondence from God, a dream or dream of blessed messengers rising and plummeting a step that came to from earth to paradise.

He wound up noticeably mindful that there really is correspondence amongst paradise and earth. He perceived in that place that God was close by, promising him direction through life, and future significance. Jehovah stated, "I am with thee, and will keep thee....and will bring thee again into this land....I won't leave thee (v.15).

What a testing message! No big surprise Jacob shouted: "The Lord is in this place... How horrendous (magnificent) is this place!" (vv.16,17) He was significantly moved. Maybe without precedent for his life he was aware of the nearness of God next to him. The voice, the encouraging statements, the real nearness of

'El Shadday conveyed him around to love and wonder and responsibility.

18-22. He called the name of the place "Beth-el," House of God, for God was there. To make this a never-to-be-overlooked understanding, he set up a stone column to demonstrate this was a blessed recognize, an asylum where hint association with God would dependably be conceivable (v.18).

Profoundly, despite everything he had far to go, yet he had gained ground in this experience with God. He additionally promised the Lord his life and a "tenth" of all belonging that would turn into his en route. Yet, he made this guarantee restrictive: If God would stay with him, keep him in the way, and bring him securely home once more, he would complete his piece of the vow.

It was a long advance forward. The "stone" (masseba) he raised would remain as a changeless indication of the promise he had made (v.22).

CHAPTER
TWENTY-NINE

Jacob's Journey
(29:1-12)

1. "Then Jacob went on his journey." The Hebrew saying, lifted up his feet, recounts the young fellow's reaction to the perfect support. He was en route to Padan-aram, looking for his mom's family close Haran. It was hard to take such a long excursion, however Jacob appeared to have no option.

Finally he remained at a well, amidst groups of sheep, with their shepherds sitting tight for the enormous stone to be taken from the mouth of the well so the sheep could be watered. Conceivably it was a similar well where Eliezer discovered Rebekah for the youthful Isaac.

In spite of the fact that numerous years had passed, Laban still lived, as Jacob gained from the shepherds, and his little girl Rachel was the attendant of his run (v. 6). At the point when Rachel drew closer with Laban's rush, Jacob ventured forward to expel the huge shake and to give water to the parched sheep.

At that point he kissed his cousin and disclosed to her his identity. Profoundly moved by all that had come upon him and by this initially meeting with kinsfolk, Jacob "lifted up his voice, and sobbed," while Rachel hurried to disclose to Laban that his nephew had arrived.

13,14. Laban, brother of Rebekah, grandson of Nahor, was thrilled to welcome one of his own bone and tissue. It had been quite a while since his sister had ridden away to wind up plainly Isaac's lady of the hour. He readily got the child of Rebekah into his family circle.

Maybe he recall the sumptuous show of riches brought by Eliezer. Maybe he was inspired by the quality of the young fellow, who may turn into a decent shepherd. More likely than not he thought about how possible it is of a spouse for his girls. Leah and Rachel were both qualified. Laban never missed a chance to drive a hard deal.

The youthful nephew from the slope nation would figure out how to bargain circumspectly with him. Truth be told, Jacob would figure out how to outmaneuver the central cheat of the considerable number of "offspring of the East."

15-20. Rachel was strangely delightful and appealing, and as of now Jacob was awed by her. The Scripture says, "Jacob cherished Rachel (v. 18). Leah, the senior sister was a long way from lovely. Her eyes did not have the radiance, shimmer, and engaging quality that men appreciate. However Leah was to be built up so immovably in sacrosanct history that succeeding eras would need to figure with her.

It would be one of her children who might be had his spot in the Messianic line. These four-Laban, Jacob, Leah, and Rachel-were to be huge figures in God's dealings with and through his picked individuals.

21-30. Subsequent to tolling seven years for the more youthful little girl, Jacob was misdirected and trap into marriage with Leah. After the wedding merriments for Leah, Jacob wedded her more youthful sister, Rachel, however needed to work seven more years as installment for her. In this manner he had two spouses of equivalent standing.

His consuming adoration for Rachel made his association with Leah rather odd and disillusioning. Leah more likely than not experienced much the acknowledgment that her better half did not love her. However she carried on with the expectation that one day Jacob's heart would swing to her.

31-35. At first neither Rachell nor Leah bore Jacob kids. Back then, to be fruitless was viewed as a terrible circumstance. Be that as it may, in time, Jehovah acted the hero and recuperated her fruitlessness, and she turned into a mother. In a steady progression her children came, until the point when she had borne six of them. A little girl, Dinah, was included for additional measure.

With disastrous normality, Leah held out a child with the words "Now my significant other will love me." But no expression of acknowledgment or thankfulness originated from Jacob. The word for "contempt" (rational) specifies "less warmth," or "less commitment." It doesn't show positive scorn.

CHAPTER
THIRTY

Rachel Also Suffered
(30:1-43)

1-13. Rachel additionally endured, for her sterile state did not enhance, and she was not bearing children for Jacob. Hebrew qane', "begrudged," has wrapped up inside it the sentiment one who has borne about everything she can stand. Begrudge, discontent, touchiness denoted her voice, her dialect, and her outward appearance. Leah, Rachel, and Jacob were all despondent.

Their residential inconvenience and despair prompted words and activities entirely unworthy, pointless, and unbecoming. Human endeavors to cure the circumstance demonstrated unsuitable. The giving of "Bilhah" and "Zilpah" as auxiliary spouses to help "manufacture" the family just ended up being pernicious.

Children were conceived however hearts were still off key and despondent. Other than Leah's six children and one girl (no less than), two children were destined to Bilhah and two to Zilpah.

14-24. Rachel tried to utilize "mandrakes" (duda'im) to instigate richness. These mandrakes were prevalently called "love apples." "The mandrake is a tuberous plant, with yellow plumlike natural product. It should go about as an adoration enchant. It ages in May, which suits the specify (v. 14) of wheat collect" (Ryle, 1914).

Rachel stayed desolate notwithstanding the superstitious charms. The circumstance was in the hands of the Lord, and he couldn't respect human endeavors to transform it. At long last, "God recollected Rachel, and God noticed to her, and opened her womb. Also, she considered, and bar a son....and she called him Joseph (vv. 22-24). In his own great time Jehovah gave his answer. He took away Rachel's "censure" and filled her with happiness and acclaim.

25-30. "Jacob said unto Laban, Send me away, that I may go....to my nation." When Joseph was conceived, Jacob had worked out in full his obligation to Laban, and he was prepared to come back to Canaan. Had he gone around then, he could have taken just his family; he didn't claim one molecule of property. He asked for his uncle to release him home.

Laban asserted to have gotten exceptional information (AV, "learned by understanding"), by enchantment or divination or from his family unit divine beings, that he should keep Jacob around to ensure achievement and flourishing.

31-36. He offered to give Jacob a chance to name his wages. Envision his unexpected when his nephew made him an offer that appeared to be overwhelmingly to support him. In Syria the sheep were white and the goats were dark, with not very many special cases.;

Jacob offered to begin in business on the double, tolerating as his the sheep that were not white and the goats that were not dark, and leaving the rest to Laban. Hence the two homes would be developed. Laban acknowledged the offer in a split second. He started "that day" by expelling to a protected separation ever accessible "offensive" sheep and goat so Jacob would have nothing with which to begin.

The isolated creatures he put in the keeping of his children. It was a low, obnoxious trap. Laban trusted that he had made it outlandish for Jacob to win, since he had taken away the majority of Jacob's capital before the challenge started.

37-42. In any case, Jacob was not to be tallied out so effectively. He introduced three gadgets to out mind his uncle. He set up streaked poles previously the ewes at the watering places that the shading of the youthful may be liable to pre-birth impact. It is a built up truth, pronounces Delitzch, that white sheep can be ensured by putting a large number of white questions about the drinking troughs (Delitzsch, 1899).

Jacob additionally isolated the spotted and striped sheep and children from the group, however kept them on display of the ewes, that they may be impacted. His third gadget was to convey these foreordaining impacts to endure upon the more grounded ewes with the goal that his sheep and children would be more grounded and more virile than the others. Jacob was savvy enough to turn to pre-birth impact and particular rearing.

43. Because of these plans, in a couple of years Jacob turned out to be hugely rich in sheep and goats. Despite the fact that he had utilize his head, he would have been the first to proclaim that the Lord interceded to five him the triumph. Jehovah was making it workable for the patriarch to come back to the guaranteed arrive with substance, and turn into the ruler of God, who might do the heavenly will.

CHAPTER
THIRTY-ONE

Jacob's Return To Canaan
(31:1-55)

1-3. "The countenance of Laban….was not toward him as before." At long last, the relations of uncle and nephew achieved the limit. Jacob saw that Laban and his children felt unfriendly toward him on account of his prosperity. Furthermore, he had sufficiently increased riches and belonging to fulfill him. Along these lines, when he got immediate walking orders from the God of Bethel, he knew the time had come to return home. Twenty years had gone, amid which time his mom had kicked the bucket. Maybe Laban would accordingly turn out to be significantly more upsetting. It was the hour for moving out.

4-13. Jacob disclosed his choice to his spouses, revealing to them how the "heavenly attendant of God" had addressed him in a fantasy and supported him in his motivation. The "holy messenger" had distinguished himself with the person who had appeared to Jacob at Bethel. He was really Jehovah himself.

14-16. Leah and Rachel firmly embraced Jacob's choice. They knew their dad, and they had lost their adoration and regard for him.

They recollected that he had gathered fourteen years of work from Jacob without giving them the part that a lady of the hour could legitimately anticipate. "Are we not checked of him outsiders?" they said. "For he hath sold us, and hath very ate up likewise our cash" (v.15).

17-21. Jacob set his rushes, groups, youngsters, and belonging in availability for the long trip, and held up until the point that Laban had left for a sheep shearing celebration. Then Rachel ensured Jacob's claim to a decent offer of the bequest by taking the "pictures" or t'rapim (cf. Latin penates), really "family divine beings," exceptionally prized by Laban. Nuzu tablets from the fifteen century B.C. demonstrate that ownership of the Nuzu denoted a man as the central beneficiary.

Obviously Rachel had not figured out how to confide in Jehovah to accommodate her needs. Jacob had neglected to show his family to trust and love God with every one of their souls. Before long Jacob and his organization moved out from Haran, crossed the Euphrates, and traveled as quickly as they could toward Canaan. Their prompt objective was the slope nation of Gilead on the eastern side of the Jordan River.

22-24. "Laban...pursued after him." After three days Laban educated of the flight. When he could get his men sorted out for interest, he was en route to overwhelm them. Despite the fact that it was an adventure of three hundred miles, he could get the escaping bunch in the slope nation of Gilead.

In transit, Laban got an unusual message from God, a charge to swear off applying any weight as a powerful influence for Jacob. He was not to talk "either great or terrible" to him, i.e., he was not to state anything. (Alternate extremes are every now and again utilized as a part of Scripture to show totality.).

25-35. Laban couldn't deflected by divine appearances. He started his opposition by communicating his awesome pain over having his little girls and amazing kids dragged away without appropriate goodbyes. All of a sudden he took after with the inquiry: "Why hast thou stolen my divine beings?" He alluded to his t'rapim (v.30; cf. 19).

Obviously Laban was more worried over losing his pictures than over losing Jacob's family. Pursuit neglected to find these little "divine beings," for Rachel had concealed them in the wicker bushel that shaped a piece of the seat on which she sat. This current "camel's furniture" (v.34) gave an Eastern woman some solace and security as she ventured.

36-55. Without a doubt Jacob discovered extraordinary help of soul in answering to Laban. The air was altogether cleared, and Laban lost the sting from his tongue. The two men made a contract with each other, approving it and celebrating the occasion by raising a pile of stones over a slope.

The pile shaped what was called "mizpah" or "standpoint point," where a watcher could see the whole nation in the two headings. It showed doubt and absence of trust. By raising such a load the men implied tha they welcomed Jehovah to sit in the post to keep watch more than two individuals who couldn't be trusted.

God was to be a sentry to watch both Laban and Jacob, with the expectation that strife may be dodged. Jacob was bound by the guarantee to treat Laban's little girls with thoughtfulness and thought. Neither of the gatherings to the agreement must pass that point to the fringe to do savagery to the next. Neither should ever move to do damage to the next, until the end of time

CHAPTER

THIRTY-TWO

Jacob's Meeting With Esau
(32:1-33:17)

1-5. "Jacob went on his way, and the angels of God met him." Both in transit out from Canaan and in transit back, these radiant envoys came to Jacob to make him aware of the eminent nearness and to guarantee him of celestial insurance. "Mahanaim," two camps, portrays an inward camp, made up of Jacob's gathering and an external organization, made up of the delivery people of God, the external organization shaping a brilliant hover of security around the voyagers. A wonderful picture of security and assurance, and peacefulness of soul! (cf. II Kgs. 6:15-17).

6-8. Esau was headed from Edom, Jacob's messengers educated him, to meet the vast organization of individuals touching base from Padan-aram. Edom was the land south of the Dead Sea, which is regularly called Seir, or Mount Seir (v.3) in the Bible. In the New Testament times individuals of Edom were called Idumaeans. Jacob had much dread in his heart as he recalled Esau's dangers of years earlier and envisioned that his sibling was making arrangements to get his requital.

"Four hundred men" under the initiative of the wild man from Edom could be unsafe. Jacob received three distinct moves to ensure security. In the first place, he went to the Lord in humble petition. Second, he sent sumptuous presents to Esau to secure his positive attitude. Third, he orchestrated his families, his belonging, and his battling men to the most ideal favorable position, and arranged to set up a decent battle in the event that it ended up noticeably essential.

9-12. In his supplication Jacob reminded the Lord that He had summoned him to influence the excursion to Canaan to and had guaranteed him assurance and triumph. The petition was true and humble, a sincere plea for security, deliverance, and assurance in the crisis that defied him.

In spite of the fact that no expression of admission approached from the solicitor's lips with respect to the wrongs he had done to Esau and Issac, Jacob modestly conceded that he was completely unworthy of God's support actually, "I am not as much as all" (v.10). He demonstrated his dread of God and confidence in him. He was actually throwing himself on the arm of the Lord for triumph and deliverance.

13-21a. The "present" (AV), or blessing minha was a detailed one, comprising of no less than 580 monsters from Jacob's decision crowds and rushes. The minha was the standard present given to a prevalent with the aim of securing support and positive attitude. Jacob stated: "I will pacify (kipper) him" (v.20). The word is a huge one in its reference to amends.

Its exacting sense is, I will cover. By methods for the blessing, Jacob planned to "cover" Esau's face with the goal that he would disregard the damage and reject his outrage. His next word-so "that he will acknowledge me"– is, truly, so tht he will lift up my face. This is representative dialect, demonstrating full acknowledgment after pardoning.

Jacob was extraordinarily unassuming, respectful, and propitiatory in his message to Esau. He called Esau "my ruler," and discussed himself as "thy hireling." He would investigate every possibility to impact compromise.

21b-23. On the night prior to Esau's landing, Jacob met the significant trial of his whole life. Subsequent to seeing his spouses and kids securely over the Jabbok, he came back toward the north bank to be separated from everyone else in the haziness. The "Jabbok" was a tributary of the Jordan, which went along with it about somewhere between the Sea of Galilee and the Dead Sea. Today the Jabbok is known as the Zerka.

24-32. "There wrestled a man with him until the breaking of the day." In the dejection of the dull night Jacob was met by a man who grappled with him. Hebrew 'abaq, to "contort," or "wrestle," has some association with the word Jabbok. After a long battle, the obscure guest requested that Jacob discharge him.

This Jacob declined to do until the outsider favored him. The 'man" requested that Jacob tell his name, which implies supplanter. At that point the outsider proclaimed that from that point on he would have another name with another importance. "Israel" can be translaated he who striveth with God, or God striveth, or he who perservereth" or, it might be related with the word sar, "sovereign."

The 'man" announced: "Thou hast endeavored with God....and hast won." It was an affirmation of triumph in managing Esau, and additionally confirmation of triumphs up and down the way. In the titanic battle, Jacob came to understand his own particular shortcoming and the prevalence of the forceful One who had touched him. Right now of yielding, he turned into another man, who could get the endowments of God and accept his place in God's arrangement.

The new name, Israel, proposes eminence and power and sway among men. He was bound to be a God-represented man rather than a corrupt supplanter. He had come through annihilation into control. All whatever is left of his life he would be injured; yet his limp would be an indication of his new eminence.

"Peniel (or Penuel) implies face of God. The I and the u are insignificant associating vowels joining the substantives pen and el. It is most likely to be situated up the Jabbok Valley around seven or eight miles from the Jordan. Jacob had seen the substance of God and still lived. He could always remember that unfathomable experience.

CHAPTER
THIRTY-THREE

Jacob Meets Esau
(33:1-30)

1-3. "Jacob lifted up his eyes, and ....behold, Esau came." At last, the snapshot of meeting arrived. Esau, with his four hundred men, came in locate. With dread and anxiety, but with is most captivating way, Jacob met his repelled sibling and prostrated himself before him seven times. Consequently, he demonstrated finish subservience.

4-11. Esau, in his reaction, uncovered a liberal and unselfish soul that was unrealistic. He had harbored threatening vibe for Jacob, and he had carried four hundred in number men alongside him as though he intended to complete his old risk. In any case, he didn't. His heart was changed. God had transformed his scorn into unselfishness.

He came to meet Jacob with comprehension and absolution. In the twenty years that had mediated, the controlling hand of God had created changes in the two men. Presently the person who had so as of late been lowered before God discovered his path smoothed out for him.

12-17. Jacob's blessing giving and Esau's excited and friendly welcome gave prove that the days ahead could bring new triumphs for God's kingdom. These men would not battle and execute each other. Despite the fact that Jacob

did not acknowledge Esau's liberal welcome to come to Mount Seir, he extraordinarily refreshing his sibling's unselfish soul.

Esau had demonstrated that he could forgive and never look back. The siblings separated in peace. At "Succoth" (stalls) Jacob, with his organization, found a home (v. 17). He really manufactured a house there. Succoth was a superb good country site on the eastern side of Jordan and north of the Jabbok.

Jacob And His Family At Shechem (33:18-34:31)

Proof is not definitive with respect to the length of Jacob's stay in Succoth. It might have been quite a while. After he made peace with Esau, he had no event to rush. Before intersection the Jordan, he most likely put in quite a while in the very much watered locale toward the east of the stream.

Intersection the stream, he ended up in the region of Shechem, where Abraham had stopped on his initially travel into the place where there is Canaan. Shechem was around forty-one miles north of Jerusalem, in the valley between Mount Ebal and Mount Gerizim.

Jacob's well was there and Sychar was not far away. Jacob purchased a package of ground in the region of Shechem, and along these lines built up claim to property in Canaan. He had been summoned to backpedal to the place that is known for this fathers and to his related, presumably meaning the region of Hebron. Absolutely he ought to have gone at any rate similar to Bethel. He was to discover that the general population of Shechem would not be an assistance to his family.

CHAPTER
THIRTY-FOUR

Jacob And His Family At Shechem
(34:1-31)

1-5. Dinah, a daughteer of Jacob and Leah, made an appalling visit to the close by city of Shechem. The youthful young lady had no foundation of profound comprehension to support her in her hour of need. Shechem, the youthful child of Hamor, fell urgently infatuated with her, and soon the awful results were known in Jacob's family.

Hebrew laqah. "took" (v. 2), demonstrates that an overwhelming power was utilized. The word ana, "debased (AV), shows shameful treatment. Poor people young lady was demolished. Promptly Shechem "addressed the heart" (v. 3) of the troubled one he had wronged, trying to support her. He cherished her and needed her for his significant other.

6-12. The word n'bala, "habit," shows a disgraceful, abhorrent, silly deed that showcases articulate apathy in moral conduct. To Jacob and his children,

Shechem's deed was a demonstration of grave shamelessness, a shock against fairness and family respect. Hamor and Shechem tried to orchestrate a marriage, since Shechem adored the young lady.

Jacob was prepared to make a concurrence with them. The mohar-pre-sent to the lady of the hour would be great. The two gatherings would be bound together so intermarriage would be legitimate.

13-24. Nonetheless, the children of Jacob were hot-headed, unwavering, and corrupt. Under the appearance of requiring religious recognition, they made the Shechemites consent to be circumcised. The greater part of the men of the tribe submitted to the ceremony.

25-29. At that point Simeon and Levi drove an assault on the city. Jacob's children chopped down every one of the men while they were debilitated for battling, and took away their families and belonging. In the historical backdrop of the patriarch's family, it is a shameful section of energy, savagery, and disfavor.

30-31. God's picked individuals in his heavenly land acted like merciless agnostics. Poor old Jacob was troubled. He reminded his children that they had made it troublesome for him to keep the positive attitude of the neighboring people groups. His mentality was unworthy of a man of confidence who was God's picked delegate to the people groups of the earth.

Narrow minded dread appear to be highest in this reasoning. He didn't reprimand his children for their unspeakable remorselessness, nor did he express distress since God's respect had been ineffectively spoken to. Jacob had put in twenty years in Laban's property, and now most likely an additional ten years in at Succoth and Shechem without doing anything significant of set up his family profoundly for the solid streams of life.

He had been excessively bustling building a material domain and increasing common favorable position to go to his youngsters' moral and profound establishments. He presently couldn't seem to achieve Bethel. Would it be past the point of no return for Dinah and Simeon and Levi and all the others? The story could make even a solid man sob.

CHAPTER

THIRTY-FIVE

The Return To Bethel
(35:1-29)

1. Jehovah articulated a grave summon to Jacob to proceed onward to his objective: "Emerge, go up to Beth-el, and stay there: and make there a holy place." Bethel was 1,010 feet higher than Shechem and arranged out and about that prompted Jerusalem, Bethlehem, and Herbon. Jacob had dawdled too long on his way to that sacred place. He was currently to construct a sacrificial stone there, as Abraham had done on his critical adventure into Palestine.

Jacob had set up a masseba, i.e., a stone column, after his never-to-be-overlooked involvement with Jehovah, when he fled toward Haran. This arrival visit in the sacred place would include a full duty of his life to the Lord. He had dismissed the sacred place of God. the profound accentuation had been missing from his reasoning and living.

2-7. Instantly and submissively, Jacob made prepared to voyage to Bethel. To start with, he approached his semipagan family to clean themselves (v. 2), to secure all terapim and noticeable portrayals of remote divine beings.

At that point the group of Jacob moved out on their sacred journey to Bethel. The general population of the spots throough which they passed were so awed by the "fear of God" that they didn't attack the pioneers (v.5).

At the point when Jacob came to "Luz," he knew he was going to stroll on blessed ground. He raised a sacred place to Jehovah and called the place "El-beth-el," the God of the place of God.

9-15. Again God appeared to Jacob and guaranteed him that his new name, Israel, would be a steady indication of his new character, his new connection to Jehovah, and his royal stroll in the perfect lifestyle. He was the beneficiary of the guarantees made to Abraham.

The pledge was still in full power, and it would keep on being official upon him and his relatives. In talking with Jacob, God utilized His name, "God Almighty, ;El-Shadday, "the all-adequate One" (v. 11). Jacob could rely on 'El-Shadday to apply any and each need, and to give the elegance for any crisis.

16-20. Presently Rachel, who had given the motivation and the affection Jacob required, arrived at the finish of her way. She passed on in bringing forth her second child, whom she named "Ben-oni," child of my sorrow. In any case, Jacob picked the name "Benjamin," child of my correct hand. Rachel more likely than not been covered some place south of Bethel, making progress toward Hebron (cf. 35:16,19).

Bethel was ten miles north of Jerusalem, and Bethlehem was around six miles south of Jerusalem. It is normally inferred that Rachel was covered in the quick region of Bethlehem. The customary sit is as yet indicated out guests to that city.

27-29. Isaac kept on living until and Jacob's arrival from Haran. From Beer-sheba he had moved to Mamre, exceptionally close to the old city of Hebron. There Abraham had obtained the Cave of Machpelah for the internment place of Sarah. Presently, at 189 years old years, "Isaac surrendered the phantom, and passed on." The single Hebrew word gawa intends to "come up short," or to "sink down."

In the hour of entombment, Esau and Jacob stood together at the grave, to respect their dad. The siblings were joined in a typical sorrow, as Ishmael and Isaac had been at the grave of Abraham.

CHAPTER
THIRTY-SIX

Edom And It's People
(36:1-43)

Before relating the biography of Joseph, the author of Genesis portrays something of the place where there is Edom and its occupants. The first occupants of Mount Seir were called Horites or Hurrians. Throughout time, Esau and his relatives assumed control over the region.

Esau progressed toward becoming wealty and had much dairy cattle and sheep. The chief urban communities of the territory were Sela, Bozrah, Petra, Teman, and Ezion-geber. The Edomites kept on being unfriendly to the Israelites all through Old Testament times (cf. Obadiah, particularly vv. 10-15).

CHAPTER

THIRTY-SEVEN

Joseph's Early Experiences
(37:1-36)

1-11. Joseph, the more seasoned child of Rachel, was a most loved of his dad Jacob. For this and different reasons he turned out to be exceedingly disagreeable with his siblings. For a certain something, he responded firmly against their exploitative and corrupt conduct, and honestly investigated them, in this way picking up for himself the name of gossip. To exacerbate the situation, his dad made for him illustrious tunics, with long, streaming sleeves, which set him out from the gathering as the favored one.

The regular induction was that Jacob had picked Joseph to be the one through whom the celestial endowments would Furthermore, Joseph dream dreams that indicated his future remarkable enormity, and he advised his fantasies to his siblings.

Jacob's children were enraged to get notification from Joseph's lips the declaration that he would lead over them. He, the youthful favored sovereign, clearly trusted that he was to have the pre-distinction over his whole family.

In his straightforward talk, he blended up every one of the flames of envy and deadly scorn. However God had as a primary concern some wondrous gifts for the chap, as time would uncover.

Joseph ought to have been guided about the best possible approach to manage blemished animals who loathed his way and his quality of predominance (as they thought). How he required an insightful advocate! Jacob clearly adored him so fervently thus indiscriminately that he couldn't manage him admirably.

12-28. The siblings harbored malevolence in their souls until the point that they resolved to dispose of Joseph. They had a lot of time to plan a plot to fulfill their motivation. From "Hebron," where they lived to Shechem in the north, these men went to discover field arrive for their groups and crowds. Jacob sent Joseph to Shechem to visit his different children and bring him expression of their welfare.

On touching base in the region of Shechem, Joseph discovered that his broothers had proceeded onward to "Dothan," around fifteen miles more distant north. At the point when the siblings saw Joseph coming, they plotted to murder him, however Reuben tried to spare the chap's life.

Reuben talked the others into placing Joseph into a reservoir, wanting to haul him out later. Judah in this way persuaded his siblings that it is shrewd to take the kid home to his dad. Judah intended to spare him from starving. As it turned out, Joseph got himself a detainee of an "organization of Ishmaelites" (v. 25) or Midianites. Before long he would be a slave in some Egyptian family. Both Ishmaelites and Midianites were relatives of Abraham. Maybe the band was comprised of men from both these people groups.

29-35. Reuben, the principal conceived, was straightforwardly in charge of the chap to his dad. Agonizingly he and the others confronted Jacob with a bloodly coat and a beguiling story that for all intents and purposes broke the core of the old patriarch. He was persuaded that his most loved child was dead. The person who, in his childhood, had been champion double crosser was currently merciless misdirected.

His misery knew no limits. He moaned: "I will go down to Sheol grieving for my child." Hebrew "Sheol" portrays the underground dwelling place the dead, offering an explanation to Greek "Hades," There, as indicated by custom, free spirits keep on existing in shadowy districts that have no exit and no correspondence with God or man. It is an insignificant half presence. Jacob understood that he would go to Sheol soon, yet he had no expectation of seeing a conclusion to his powerful sufferings until that hour.

36. "The Ishmaelites" sold Joseph to "Potiphar,: an authority in the court of Pharaoh. Clearly Potiphar was the "head of the killers. The word most likely alluded to crafted by butchering creatures utilized for give up. The young Joseph was named steward of Potiphar's living arrangement. He was far from home and apparently, significantly more remote far from the acknowledgment of his paradise sent longs for pre-greatness.

Be that as it may, Joseph's God was all the while working out his motivations and plans. What's more, he was going to utilize Potiphar and Pharooah to propel his heavenly program.

CHAPTER

THIRTY-EIGHT

Judah And Tamar
(38:1-30)

Amidst the story portraying Joseph's vocation in Egypt, the author of Genesis presents the record of Judah's dishonorable inclusion among the Canaanites. Judah was the main individual from Jacob's family, one foreordained too be the channel of all Jehovah's rich guarantees to and through Abraham to later eras and the world. Judah's name was to be unmistakable in the Messianic line. David would be one of his regarded relatives.

2-11. "Judah saw ....a daughter of a certaom Canaanite, whose name was Shuah; and he took her." This sidelight on family life in Canaan uncovers to what profundities of corruption a few, at any rate, of the Chosen People had fallen. Judah wedded the little girl of Shuah, an agnostic Canaanite, and in this manner began a chain of wicked occasions. Two children, Er and Onan, passed on without leaving youngsters.

Judah guaranteed Tamar, who had been the spouse of the siblings, in a steady progression, that she ought to have his third child, Shelah, for a husband, when he happened to the correct age. The family line must not vanish.

12-23. In time, when Tamar understood that her dad in-law was not staying faithful to his commitment, she took things into her own hands. Putting on a show to be one of the kedeshot (religious whores), she deceived Judah into having illegal relations with her.

24-26. At the point when Judah discovered that Tamar was pregnant, he proclaimed her deserving of death, just to find that he was the blameworthy father of her tyke. He stated: "She hath been more honorable than I (AV).

27-30. The record of the corner of the twins, "Perez" and "Zerah," closses the section. The differentiation amongst Joseph and his senior sibling would be all the more sharp when Joseph uncovered his conduct in his hour of enticement. Judah expected to wind up noticeably another man to please in the Lord's sight.

CHAPTER

THIRTY-NINE

Joseph And The Wife Of Potiphor
(39:1-23)

1-6b. "And Joseph was brought down to Egypt." At the point when Joseph took up his work at Potiphor's home, he was a slave and an outsider. In the first place, he turned into an individual orderly to the Egyptian officer. At the point when Potiphar discovered him ready, fast, and reliable, and saw that "the Lord" was with him (v. 3), he set him over the whole foundation as his put stock in supervisor.

In his new position Joseph was in charge of everything about the administration of the house, with one special case: As a nonnative, he couldn't see to the planning of nourishment (cf. 43:32).

6c. Joseph was uncommonly alluring. He resembled his mom, Rachel, of whom it was said; "Rachel was lovely and all around favored," "reasonable in frame" and "reasonable in looks" (cf. 29:17). What's more Joseph transmitted a sweet, clean piety that made him much additionally engaging.

7-13. Potiphar's significant other couldn't avoid the impulse to make a success of Joseph.

Evidently she didn't have anything to involve her psyche and no standards to undergird her in the hour of allurement. For Joseph who lived continually in fellowship with the heavenly God to sin with the lady was totally impossible. It would have been sin against God, and out of line to the man who believed him so implicity.

Despite the fact that the enticement accompanied unobtrusive, sudden, solid interest, Joseph's triumph was guaranteed.

14-20. Baffled, the seductress turned into a slanderer. In a wrath she went forward to blame Joseph dishonestly for underhanded goal, planning to mix up sensitivity with respect to different workers, and to make her better half sufficiently irate to slaughter the young fellow. The conditional confirmation was unequivocally implicating. Potiphar was rankled. Nonetheless, disregarding the reality of the charge, he clearly had some inquiry in his brain about Joseph's blame, for he didn't murder him.

Rather, he rushed him off to the "jail" (the "Round House:). This jail was most likely a well known round pinnacle or cell where detainees associated with official life were housed. The

Hebrew sohar, jail, might be an endeavor to interpret an Egyptian word.

In the Egyptian Tales of Two Brothers, there is an intriguing parallel to the experience of Joseph. In that story a man who was hitched lived in a similar house with his sibling. The spouse of the primary man blamed the more youthful sibling for shameful advances. The spouse, however infuriated, looked to know reality about the issue. On discoveries his better half blameworthy, the spouse executed her. This story goes back to the times of Seti II, that is, to around 1180 B.C.

21-23. Life in jail was not alluring, but rather the story announces that "the Lord was with" Joseph. What a distinction that made! He was empowered to appreciate comfort and strength.

CHAPTER

FORTY

Joseph's Prison Experiences
(40:1-23)

1-4. "The Butler ….and ….baker had offended their lord the king of Egypt…. And Pharaoh ….put them in ward. Indeed, even in the jail Joseph couldn't be kept down. He was given supervision of the detainees, and "he served unto them." The old prison turned into a better place as a result of his essence. God was favoring others through Joseph's keenness and generosity. Potiphar had put him where his noteworthy abilities could at present be felt.

The "head servant" (mashgeh), or drink-supplier, was an esteemed individual from Pharaoh's family unit. In Neh. 1:11 the word is interpreted "cupbearer." Nehemiah who bore that title, was a confided in official in the royal residence of the Persian ruler. the "cook" (opeh) was the administrator of the bread shop, in charge of making sure that the ruler's sustenance was sheltered and satisfactory. These two high authorities in the regal family had affronted Pharaoh.

Pending examination, they were kept in a similar jail to which Joseph had been submitted.

5-23. It was the obligation of the youthful Hebrew to tend to these two detainees. Discovering them furious and aggravated, he asked concerning their requirements. They had imagined that they couldn't get it. Furthermore, no official translator of dreams was accessible.

Joseph advised them that God could give the importance. At that point they disclosed to him their fantasies, and he clarified what they connoted. The head servant would have a wonderful amazement: Within three days he would be allowed an official discharge from jail to backpedal to his work at the lord's side. The pastry specialist would be discharged in the meantime, however his head would be separated from his body and his remains would be hung out in the open to end up sustenance ridiculous.

Joseph influenced one demand of the head servant; "To have me in they rememberance when it might be well with thee, and shew kindness....and go on about me unto Pharaoh (v 14). Joseph needed to be allowed to live and help realize the full will of God in his life.

CHAPTER

FORTY-ONE

Joseph And Pharaoh
(41:1-57)

1-8. "At the end of two years…. Pharaoh dreamed; and, behold, he stood by the river. The king envisioned that he remained by the Nile (y'or), the supplier of life and refreshment to the ground. (The nation relied upon the waterway to give paradise sent water system a seemingly endless amount of time). Furthermore, he saw seven very much bolstered cows nibbling in a glade. By and by seven thin dairy cattle went along and gobbled up the fatter ones.

Once more, he saw seven great ears of grain on one stalk, and seven poorer ones showed up and ate up them. These fantasies profoundly distrubed Pharaoh, particularly when no man could be found to intepret them. The "performers (hartummim) were the consecrated copyists who had more information of the mysterious than some other insightful men in the domain.

Be that as it may, even they were bewildered and defenseless this time. Their unique preparing in the holy secrets demonstrated deficient for deciphering these fantasies. What did everything mean? the lord pondered. Who could let him know?

9-24. All of a sudden the central head servant recalled Joseph, subsequent to having overlooked him for a long time, and advised Pharaoh of his capacity to translate dreams. Rapidly the youthful Hebrew was summoned. In a short time he showed up at the royal residence, shaved and impeccably dress. Pharaoh said he had heard that Joseph icy translate dreams, however Joseph made it very obvious that the elucidation must originate from the Lord: "God should give Pharaoh an answer of Peace (AV, v.16).

25-32. Decisively and with bizarre clearness, the young fellow uncovered to the ruler that his fantasies predicted seven years of bounty, to be trailed by seven years of wrecking starvation. The prior time of seven years would be a period of ripeness and plentiful harvests. The starvation years would bring need and enduring and passing.

33-36. "Look out a man discreet and wise." Joseph went past negligible translation and gave some practical counsel. No time was to be lost. An insightful man of unrivaled capacity must be discovered who could direct horticultural creation, father gigantic stores of grain, and, in due time, make savvy air of the amassed assets. The position would request the best man the kingdom could bear.

37-42. Fortunately, Pharaoh was an insightful man, for he perceived Joseph as a "man in whom the soul of God" was (v. 38). He made him the sustenance manager of Egypt, and designated him the stupendous vizier or head administrator. He set him in summon over the whole kingdom, beside himself.

He had his own seal ring set on Joseph's hand, as an identification of specialist, engaging him to issue official orders. He had him dressed in uncommon articles of clothing saved for Egypt's mightiest men, and an extraordinary recognized administration chain set about his neck.

43. Joseph was to ride in a chariot and be viewed as second just to the ruler. A unique authority would shout to the general population, "Abrek!" This most likely signified, "Focus!" or "Bow the knee." (AV), or something comparative. It was to be clarified to every one of the general population that a remarkable man

of capacity, character, and specialist was before them. He was to be in entire control of issues that implied desperate to hoards.

Benefit and duty competed with each other at the time of acknowledgment and venture. The testing expressions of Mordecai to Esther may well have been addressed Joseph: "Who knoweth whether thou workmanship go to the kingdom for such a period as this?" (Est. 4:4, AV).

45, 46, 50-52. Joseph was "thirty years of age when he stood before Pharaoh," having been in Egypt for twelve or thirteen years. From the jail to the royal residence in one day was a compelling advance. God, who had been with the young fellow each moment of his life, had accommodated this jump. Next, Pharaoh gave Joseph an Egyptian name – "Zaphnath – paa'neah (which in the Coptic, as per a few researchers, implies "a revealer of insider facts," or, "the man to whom privileged insights are uncovered"; cf. AV marg.).

He likewise gave him a spouse named "Asenath," who was from one of the holy families, her dad being "ruler," or "minister of On." "On," a city of culture and religion arranged around seven miles north of Cairo, was the focal point of sun love. To Asenath and Joseph were conceived two children. Manasseh and Ephraim, These young men, a few years after the fact, were freely embraced into the tribe of Jaacob, and progressed toward becoming heads of two tribes in Israel.

CHAPTER

FORTY-TWO

The First Visit Of The Brothers
(42:1-38)

1-8. And Joseph's ten brethren went down to buy corn in Egypt....But Benjamin....Jacob sent not with his brethren....lest....mischief befall him. At the point when starvation ended up plainly serious in Canaan, and starvation appeared to be unavoidable, Jacob realized that sustenance must be secured somewhere else. He sent his ten children to Egypt to purchase grain. Benjamin he kept at home to be a solace to him. At the point when the ten siblings introduced themselves before the "senator" of Egypt to purchase grain, they didn't remember him as their sibling.

At least twelve years had slipped by. The thin youth they had sold had developed into a man. He remained before them now as the mightiest figure in the place that is known for Egypt. His dialect, his dress, his official bearing, and his position did their part in camouflaging him. Be that as it may, Joseph perceived his siblings without a moment's delay.

9-12. When he blamed his siblings for being spies, he was however point out their the most clear clarification of their coming. Egyptians understood that their eastern outskirt was particularly helpless, thus they dreaded Asiatic people groups. Joseph blamed the ten men for coming to Egypt to find the frail places in the outskirt safeguards keeping in mind the end goal to offer data to would-be intruders.

13-24. At the point when the men recounted their dad and youthful sibling, he requested verification of their trustworthiness. On of them, he stated, must go home to convey the most youthful child to Egypt while the others stayed in jail. In the wake of keeping the men in "ward" for three days, Joseph recommended the less demanding arrangement of holding one of them as a prisoner while the other nine ran home with the grain. "Simeon" was chosen to stay in jail (v. 24). He was Jacob's second child, and convention holds that he was the most pitiless of the considerable number of siblings.

21-24. Throughout the discussion, Joseph saw that his siblings were significantly concerned and contrite. He detected their devotion to Jacob and their strong family soul. "He....wept" as he thought of the days of yore and the agony the men had caused by their antagonistic vibe and mercilessness, and as he perceived their difference in heart.

25-38. In transit back to Canaan, one of Jacob's children made the exasperating disclosure that his cash was in the highest point of his grain sack. Furthermore, when the gathering achieved home and discharged their sacks they found "each man's....money" in his sack. They were astounded and frightened by this revelation.

The puzzle of the cash, the confinement of Simeon, and the news that the Egyptian senator was requesting to see Benjamin-all were excessively for the great matured Jacob. His despondency and dread practically overpowered him. What's more, he would not consent to release his most youthful child back with the others to Egypt.

CHAPTER
FORTY-THREE

Further Experiences With The Brothers (43:1-34)

1-14. "When they had eaten up the corn …. their father said …. Go again, buy us a little food" (v. 2). The men guaranteed their dad that they challenged not go to Egypt without Benjamin's well-being, would Jacob release his most youthful child. Judah stated: "Send the fellow with me …. "I will be surety for him. Judah really swore his own life to ensure the sheltered return of Benjamin (cf. 44:32-34). Without a doubt the children of Jacob had adapted much since the day they had looked to kill Benjamin's sibling.

At the point when Jacob saw that Benjamin needed to go, he guided his children to set up an abundant minha, "exhibit" (v. 11), for "the man" – a portion of the best nectar, the choicest organic products, the rarest nuts, and other of the best delights of the land. He likewise guided them to reclaim twofold the cash they had found in their sacks.

Most likely the second part of cash was to be utilized to pay for the grain they were to buy this time. Before sending his children away, Jacob supplicated that "God Almighty" ('El Shadday) may keep them and supply each need (v. 14).

15-34. When they touched base in Egypt, they were startled to find that they were to go to the senator's home to eat. The new bewildered and frightened them. They expected that some unpleasant discipline was to be gone by upon them, for they didn't recognize what's in store from the fabulous vizier of Egypt. At the point when the considerable man went into the room where they were, they "bowed themselves to him to the earth" in full reverence (v. 26).

Joseph treated them generous and charitably, giving a dinner to them, at which he showered additional endowments on Benjamin. He got himself effectively mixed as he had association with them. It was an event the siblings couldn't overlook. They devoured and drank generally. When the supper was finished, Joseph knew the men much better; he realized that they had changed!

CHAPTER

FORTY-FOUR

Judah's Sacrificial Proposal
(44:1-34)

Joseph had one last test for his siblings, one ascertained to give him an unmistakable photo of their inward hearts.

1-5. He requested his steward to set up the sacks of grain as earlier and place his silver flagon or bowl taken care of Benjamin would convey. "Put each man's cash in his sack's mouth. Furthermore, put my container .... in the sack's mouth of the most youthful." This challis was a "divining container" (cf. v. 5), a prized ownership, utilized for accepting prophets or pictures of coming occasions.

To begin with, water was poured in. At that point little pieces of gold, silver, or valuable stones were tossed into the water. At the point when the water was shaken marginally, the pieces framed a "photo" or example. Gifted clients of the gadget guaranteed to have the capacity to divine the obscure. It was a class of enchantment called "hydromancy."

6-13. Joseph had the brothers captured as they set out on their trip toward Canaan. They challenged their guiltlessness and readily acknowledged the choice that the liable individual ought to stay in Egypt as a slave forever. Incredibly, the flagon was found in Benjamin's sack!

Brought before Joesph, they were puzzled with dread and gloom. What could any of them do? Reuben, Benjamin, and the others were noiseless.

14-34. At that point Judah represented himself and his siblings in one of the brilliant articulations of writing. He offered no reason, made no disavowal, however just pled with the strong Egyptian authority for the life and flexibility of Benjamin. This request was "the most total example of authentic normal expressiveness hopeful in any dialect." The soul of selflessness, once so unfamiliar to Judah, shone forward with uncommon magnificence.

Judah honestly admitted his own particular sins and the transgressions of his siblings. Certainly, they had not stolen the grain cash nor the divining container, however they had submitted the dark sin of offering their sibling into bondage. They had caused Joseph and their dad unspeakable melancholy and anguish. By his references to his dad's affliction, Judah uncovered himself as one now distinctly mindful of hallowed esteems and connections.

The more seasoned sibling's' ability to wind up plainly a substitute for Benjamin marks him as an awesome soul. He offered himself as Joseph's worker, and asked that Benjamin and his different siblings may be sent home to favor the core of the old father. This was the peak of God's dealings with Judah. The Lord had made in him an otherworldly champion to speak to Him in working out the perfect arrangement.

CHAPTER
FORTY-FIVE

Joseph's Invitation To Jacob
(45:1-28)

1-8. Joseph could not refrain himself....And he wept aloud....And —said unto his brethren, I am Joseph. At the point when Joseph could never again limit his emotions, he gave forward his voice in sobbing (actually). In a minute he had unveiled his distinguish and opened his awesome heart to his siblings. They, in their disarray and dread, were puzzled. Be that as it may, Joseph consoled them. He announced: "God sent me before you to safeguard life (v. 5). He rapidly too from their shooulders all the fault for a revolting deed, as he looked to decipher to them the arrangement and motivation behind God. It was his method for fixating their consideration on the one preeminent thought.

The fortunate design was more noteworthy than any minor demonstration of mortal man. That reason included safeguarding alive a leftover who could be utilized to work out the Lord's will in the earth.

9-24. Joseph asked his brethren to convey father and come to Egypt to live. He clarified that the starvation would last five more years, however that in Egypt he could give a home and boundless supplies for Jacob and the whole family gathering. They could settle in "the place where there is Goshen," which was around forty miles from the site of present-day Cairo.

Arranged in the delta of the Nile, this segment was the best of the land for crowds and rushes. It was close On and furthermore Memphis, where Joseph lived. At the point when the siblings set out for home, he sent wagons alongside them for the arrival with grain, introduces, and supplies of different types.

25-28. As the old patriarch Jacob tuned in to his children's report, "murmur heart wound up noticeably numb" (swooned, AV), for he couldn't trust the uplifting news about his missing child (v. 26). Be that as it may, when he saw the wagons and shows, and heard "Joseph's message" to him, his soul resuscitated and he started to anticipate joining his child in Egypt. It was a day of solace and celebrating for one who had seen much misery.

CHAPTER
FORTY-SIX

The Migration To Egypt
(46:1-34)

1-4. "Israel took his journey…. And came to Beer-sheba." Jacob in all likelihood was inhabiting Hebron right now. His initially stop on his earth shattering trip to Egypt was at Beersheba. There he offered penances, and there, in a night vision, God addressed him, empowering him in his turn and guaranteeing him of uncounted gifts.

To begin with, he recharged the guarantee that Jacob's relatives would turn into an awesome country. He influenced it to clear that Egypt was to be where this expansion would occur.

Second, he stated: "I will go down with thee," therefore ensuring assurance and security. Third, he stated: "I will…bring thee up." This forecast was bound to be satisfied after Jacob's demise, in the Exodus, when the forceful hand of God would convey His anointed ones from the energy of Egypt and take them back to Canaan. The affirmation that Joseph would "put his hand upon" Jacob's eyes was a prediction that the distinguished child would play out the last ceremonies at his dad's passing.

5-28. Empowered by the message from the Lord, Jacob moved out, with his relatives, from Beer-sheba and continued on the long trip to the place where there is Goshen. He picked Judah to go ahead of time of the organization ("sent Judah before him....to direct his face unto Goshen," AV), to meet Joseph and finish the game plans for their passage into the land.

29,30. The meeting of Jacob and Joseph was a moment of awesome joy. Both were too profoundly moved to talk. They held each other in a solid grasp for a "decent time" (v. 29). At the point when the old patriarch could talk, he stated: "Now let me kick the bucket, since I have seen thy confront, that thou workmanship yet alive (v. 30). He had encountered the highest delight of life.

31-34. Before Joseph introduced his family to Pharaoh, he gave them particular bearings about how to answer to the ruler's inquiries. At the point when gotten some information about their calling, they were to speak to themselves as shepherds. At that point Pharaoh would likely allot them the place where there is Goshen as their home. Goshen would give incredible brushing to their groups and crowds. They would be as one, and in this manner all around shielded from blending with different people groups.

CHAPTER
FORTY-SEVEN

Jacob And Pharaoh
(47:1-12)

1-6. "Then Joseph...told Pharaoh.... My father and my brethren — are come." The meeting with Pharaoh was paramount. Five of the siblings, decided for the reason by Joseph, exhibited to the ruler the demand that Goshen may be alloted to them, since they were shepherds. The ruler concurred that they ought to be settled around there, where touching was taking care of business.

He additionally solicited Joseph to name some from the best men among them, "men of action" (v. 6)), to be given spots of duty among his cattlemen. Egypt spent much cash and exertion in reproducing fine dairy cattle.

7-10. The peak of the event was Joseph's introduction of his matured father to the ruler. "Jacob favored Pharaoh" (v. 7). The word barak, showing up twice, might be deciphered saluted, yet the typical and unequivocally favored significance is "honored."

Right then and there the solid godly man remained before the immense ruler with pride and in the cognizance that he himself was the agent of the Almighty ('El Shadday). What could have been more normal for him than to present a paradise sent gift on the ruler of Egypt.

He realized that he held a wonderful position in God's program. With calm respect he talked the sacred gift upon Pharaoh. Jacob was an exceptional channel of awesome favors, and Pharaoh was the beneficiary.

At the point when asked his age, the patriarch answered. "The times of my staying (gur) are a hundred and thirty years" (v. 9). His life had been set apart by a progression of wanderings. It appeared to be short to him in examination with the more extended existences of Abraham and Isaac.

11,12. "The land of Rameses" was related to the place that is known for Goshen. The eastern piece of the delta of the Nile contained a territory that incorporated the place of the renowned city worked by Rameses in a later era. "Joseph supported (yekalkel) his dad." The specific type of the verb Kul utilized here (the pilpel) may signify "to feed," "to maintain," or "to ensure." It is evident that Joseph did these things in giving rich care and love to Jacob.

The Food Administrator
(47:13-27)

As starvation conditions deteriorated, the Egyptians fell into desperate need. the Scripture says, "There was no bread in all the land." The general population came to Joseph looking for nourishment for their families. At the point when their cash gave out, they exchanged their dairy cattle for grain (v. 17). At long last, they needed to vow their territories and their bodies to Pharaoh with a specific end goal to secure more sustenance (v. 19).

Hence, every one of the grounds of the domain, aside from the property of the clerics, go under the control of Pharaoh. An undeniable medieval framework appeared. The administration outfitted the general population seed, and the general population paid 20 for every penny of their respect the state (vv. 23b, 24). It was a troubling circumstance, however the general population consented to it with a specific end goal to eat.

They said to Joseph: "Thou hast spared our lives.... we will be Pharaoh's hirelings (v. 25)."

The extraordinary crisis had made intense measures vital. Thus the general population of Egypt moved toward becoming serfs, and their territory turned into the property of the state.

Jacob And The Sons Of Joseph
(47:28-31)

29,30. "And the time drew nigh that Israel must die." Jacob experienced his declining a long time in peace, bounty, and satisfaction. Prior to the finish of his life he influenced Joseph to guarantee to take his body back to Canaan for entombment. His lif had been a tumultuouss one; he had meandered far. Yet, he needed his bones covered adjacent to those of Abraham, Isaac, Sarah, Rebekah, and Leah. The "covering place" specified by Jacob was the buckle of Machpelah acquired by Abraham at the season of Sarah's passing (cf. Gen. 23).

The body of Jehovah's picked delegate would be let go with those of alternate patriarchs. As indicated by the account (v.31), Jacob turned over all over and extended with the goal that his head was at the leader of the bed. Therefore he modestly and respectfully prostrated himself.

The other rendering, bowed himself on the highest point of his staff, has nothing to laud it over the Masoretic content.

Before Jacob passed on, he embraced Joseph's two sons. Manasseh and Ephraim, and hence raised them to the level of his own children. Along these lines, when the guaranteed arrive was alloted to the tribes numerous years after the fact, Joseph was spoken to by two full offers. In this way Rachel turned into the mother of three tribes in the kingdom of Israel.

CHAPTER
FORTY-EIGHT

Joseph's Two Boys Received Jacob's Benediction (48:1-14)

Joseph conveyed his two young men to his dad to got his invocation. He masterminded his children so Jacob's correct hand would rest upon Manasseh, the senior kid, and his left hand upon Ephraim. Be that as it may, however Jacob was old and practically visually impaired, he intentionally rectified the positions by laying his correct hand on the leader of the more youthful and his left hand on Manasseh.

He recognized what he was doing. At the point when Joseph tried to change his dad's hands with the goal that Manasseh would get the head favoring (as per custom), he was educated that Ephraim was bound to get it (v. 19). The patriarch's grave gift talked upon the children of Joseph was an official as a last will and confirmation. In it Jacob incorporated a forecast of future unmistakable quality for each of the young men, yet Ephraim's development and viability was to be a long ways past Manasseh's'.

15-22. At the point when the matured man came to articulate an extraordinary gift upon Joseph, her alluded to God in a triple title: The God of our fathers, the God who shepherded me, and the Angel of deliverance. In this manner, the hereditary, the individual, and the redemptive parts of God were spoken to. Hebrew ro'eh (AV, encouraged) conveys shepherding (cf. Ps. 23:1). "The Angel which recovered me from all shrewd" (AV, v. 16) distinguishes this One with the Angel of Jehovah who ameliorated Hagar (16:7; 21:17) and who cautioned Abraham of the approaching pulverization of Sodom (Gen. 18); as it were, this "Blessed messenger" was simply the Lord in his Old Testament sign.

Jacob said that Joseph was to have the uncommon 'shoulder' (sh'kem) or mountain slant of surprising worth (AV, "one portion above thy brethren). This presumably alludes to the property Jacob had gained from Hamor, in spite of the fact that Genesis 34 demonstrate that Jacob revoked the way in which it was first taken. It was most likely recovered by Jacob later from the Amorites (cf. In 4:5).

CHAPTER

FORTY-NINE

The Solemn Blessing
(49:1-27)

1,2. "Jacob called unto his sons, and said, Gather yourselves together…... and hear."

In his goodbye deliver to his children, Jacob rose to the abnormal stature of a prophet talking in the idyllic dialect of motivation. He summoned every child thus to his bedside to hear expressions of gift, of scold, or of revile. For each situation he singled out some striking attribute of character as his evaluation of the man and his family gathering.

Jacob's words constituted a forecast of future advancements in light of the father's learning of the character of every child. The men comprehended their dad's serious expressions to be critical and determinative expectations.

3,4. "Reuben," the main conceived of Leah, had appreciated pre-greatness among his siblings. Be that as it may, he relinquished his common rights. His place as the favored first-conceived was given to Joseph. His benefits as cleric were to go to the children of Levi. His entitlement to be the leader of the tribes of Issrael, i.e., his royal right, would go to Judah.

Consequently Reuben, enriched with nobility, first-conceived rights, and common excellencies, would relinquish each place of influence and impact on account of the precariousness of his character. His unspeakable sin with Bilhah gave confirmation of good shortcoming that spelled demolish.

His uncontrolled enthusiasm (AV, insecure as water) is envisioned in the Hebrew as "dilute without restriction pouring in a frothing deluge" (v. 4). Despite the fact that equipped for dreams and plans and great aims, he couldn't be relied on to bring them through to finish.

5-7. "Simeon and Levi," Jacob's second and third children by Leah, were siblings in savagery. The old father would always remember their brutal slaughter of the Shechemites. They uncovered their actual characters that day, for they viciously assaulted and obliterated men they had beforehand made defenseless by system and double dealing.

Around then they were scolded by their dad. Presently, as he lay on his passing bed, they heard the gnawing expressions of his revile: "I will separate them in Jacob and disperse them in Israel" (v. 7b).

They were not to have an area they could call their own, yet would be scattered among alternate tribes. In Canaan this revile was satisfied: The Simeonites were swalled up into the tribe of Judah; the Levites had no region alloted to them, yet filled in as clergymen of the asylum and instructors of Israel.

8-10. "Judah," Jacob's fourth child by Leah, got the primary inadequate acclaim from the old patriarch. He conveyed the expectation of Israel upon his individual. Having neither bequest nor extraordinary respect nor profound forces, he would rise as the effective pioneer of a people who could energetically appreciate and applaud him. (Judah implies applaud.) He would be dreaded by his foes, for as a lion he would seek after them tirelessly until the point when triumph was his.

At that point, having finished his central goal, he would resign to his mountain speed to rest in the security of a fortification that none could take. He would get a handle on in his grasp the sceptor or cudgel that would symbolize his authority in the parts of warrior, lord, and judge. Any country could be cheerful, secure, and respected with Judah as its head and defender.

11,12. Peace, bounty and flourishing would win in Judah's property. The vines would be so thriving and the grapes so plentiful that the overcoming rider could attach his stallion's reins to the huge branches and appreciate the delectable natural product. The wine would be plentiful to the point that men could wash their garments in it, on the off chance that they picked.

The decision grapes would give the finest sustenance. Judah's eyes would not be red with intemperate drinking ("red with wine," v 12, AV) yet splendid with thriving' and his teeth would be "more white than drain" (AV, "white with drain). That is, Judah's property would be supernaturally honored.

The expression, "until the point that Shiloh come," was talked by Jacob amidst his prophetic photo of Judah's place in the arrangement of God. For us, the abnormal sparkle his expectation is incredibly upgraded by the way that from antiquated circumstances it has been viewed as a Messianic message.

The Hebrew might be rendered either, "until the point when Shiloh come," or till he comes whose it is. In either rendering the essential reference must be to Judah, in any case the Messiah is the genuine one who should come. As it were, the power could never leave from Judah until the point that He came who had a privilege to rule. The forecast, until the point that he come whose correct it is, is rehashed in Ezk. 21:27.

In the event that this elucidation is right, at that point Jacob's words here constitute one of the most punctual appearances of the Messianic guarantee. That which Jacob empowered to see was an unmistakable photo of Judah's legacy. Yet, the full acknowledgment of God's motivations would not be delighted in until the perfect ruler, the Messiah, showed idealize sway.

Luckily, the OT presents an unmistakable line of predictions starting at Gen. 3:15 and proceeding through the Psalms and the Prophets-with respect to the Messiah's' coming to rule as King of rulers. Jacob considered Judah to be the father of the regal tribe that would apply power and initiative over all the others. Through disasters and troublesome circumstances, God would make sure that the staff would stay in the tribe of Judah until the thoughts ruler, the Messiah, would come.

13. "Zebulun," Jacob's 6th child by Leah, was to be arranged in a place where business action and thriving would be conceivable. This may imply that domain along the seacoast was to be designated to the tribe of Zebulun. Or, on the other hand, it might imply that success would go to the relatives of Zebulun in light of their proximately to the Phoenicians, who had boundless access to the exchange courses.

Jacob notices "Sidon" as being there. it is likewise conceivable that Jacob's forecast was not completely done when the last division of the land was made. In the tune of Deborah (Jud. 5) the general population of Zebulun are warmly praised for their valorous remain against Sisera and his armed force.

14,15. "Issachar," Jacob's fifth child by Leah, is spoken to as a strrong, bull like admirer of rest and calm. The word hamor, truly, hard ass, does not allude to the will, armada, brave creature that would get the attention of the on looker. In actuality, it assigns a capable large animal weight that submits himself to the irritating burden without grievance all together that he might be allowed to lie discreetly in straightforwardness and solace.

In this way Jacob was anticipating that the tribe of Issachar would submit to the Canaanite trespasser, who might affix the burden upon them. Rather than battling, the men of this tribe would docilely enable themselves to end up slaves of the general population of the land. They would incline toward disgrace and subjection to brave activity.

16-18. "Dan," The main child of Bilhah, would turn into a solid protector of his won individuals. He would argue their motivation and guard and help them in their battle for autonomy. The tribe would be little, however they would be extraordinarily dreaded by neighbors who may try to trample upon them.

Jacob called Dan a horned snake in the way (AV "a serpent incidentally, v. 17), to cause dread and perpetrate fast lethal injuries. Hebrew nahash implies a snake in the grass, as well as a venomous reptile with dangerous teeth. That is Dan would be exceedingly unsafe to his adversaries.

In later circumstances individuals from the tribe of Dan satisfied these words with momentous exactness. After a period in their unique region, the Danites moved toward the north and involved the northernmost point in Israel. These individuals were never recognized for their otherworldly achievements. In 931 B.C. Jeroboam set up a brilliant calf in Dan to give chance to agnostic love.

19. "Gad" was the primary child of Leah's handmaid, Zilpah. The age patriarch perceived that the overcome, warlike soul of Gad would be a solid help to his kin in the life in Canaan. Jacob anticipated that Gad would require all his guile, bravery, and determination in battling, in light of the fact that he would be pestered by the ceaseless assaults of abandon tribes. Ravaging groups would push downward on him meaning a troop-to demonstrate the fierceness and brutality of the bandits from the betray.

He anticipated that Gad would be successful and would have the capacity to push the adversary away. After the victory of Palestine, the tribe of Gad was positioned east of the Jordan.

20. "Asher," Zilpah's second child, conveyed a name meaning upbeat. Jacob imagined him in a rich field, where wheat and wine and oil

would be delivered in plenteous measure. He would be prosperous and would pick up wealth. The rarities he would deliver would be fit for the table of a lord. (Indeed, even the rulers of Tire and Sidon would want them). The tribe of Asher wwitnessed the satisfaction of that male centric prediction.

21. "Naphtali, the second child of Bilhah, would exhibit a striking adoration for flexibility; he was a "rear let free," Jacob said. The outline depicts a wild, quick, agile creature that takes pleasure in the opportunity gave by lush slopes and open valleys. Naphtali was to have the keep running of God's awesome outside.

"He giveth goodly words is, maybe a reference to the persuasive and supportive talks that would continue from the mouths of men of this tribe. Barak, due to his valor, wound up plainly one of their prize shows. In Jud. 5:18 we read: Zebulum and Naphtali were a people that hazarded their lives unto the demise."

22. "Joseph," the principal child of Rachel, got the most noteworthy acclaim of the considerable number of children. A man of vision, dreams, of good and otherworldly quality, he exemplified every one of that was

best in the domain of Old Testament living. In his few parts as child, sibling, slave, and adminstrator, he showed his better character through his steadfast devotion than God. Jacob called Joseph "a youthful organic product tree." Hebrew para (AV, fruitful bough) contains a play on the name "Ephraim." The reference is to an overwhelmingly developing tree or vine, implying imperativeness and energy. As a result of being planted by a bubbling fountain (AV, well), it would continue to grow and bear fruit.

In the dry nation, water had the effect amongst sterility and productivity. Dampness ensured fruitfulness. A tree so reinforced could be relied upon to toss its branches or its rings over the divider in giving its copious organic product to the people groups of the earth.

23. Because of his uncommon success, Joseph could expect intense envy and threatening vibe. "The toxophilite" would be occupied in their incensed assaults. This had been valid in Joseph's before days, when his siblings, disenchanted by begrudge, looked to annihilate him. Numerous years after the fact, in the place that is known for Canaan, the tribes of Ephraim and Manasseh would experience

resistance and mistreatment. They would need to have a living confidence in Jehovah of hosts, who had substantiated himself the all-adequate God.

Joseph knew him and had inclined toward him in each crisis. "Woefully lamented .... shot at .... despised," interpret three Hebrew words. Marar, in the piel fom, intends to "incite," "disenthrall," "bug." The utilization of this piel frame, in addition to the word rebab adds to the force of the activity and discusses its rehashed event. The third word, satam, conveys the possibility of profound situated contempt, alongside dynamic oppression.

24,25. "His bow dwelling place quality." In Joseph's triumphs there had been confirmations of the firm bow and the spry hands, the exceptional power given by the Lord. Jacob anticipated that this same extraordinary help could be normal on the slopes of Palestine.

The word deciphered firm or "dwelling place quality," could well be rendered unaffected, persevering, or regularly streaming. Jacob utilized the titles, "Compelling One of Jacob ... the God of thy father, and the Almighty ('El Shadday), to depict the arm that would be so intense, so tried and true, so fast and deft that no enemy could oppose it.

In basic confidence he endowed the tribe of Joseph into divine hands, and in sure confidence he prognosticated certain triumphs over the adversaries who anticipated them. Notwithstanding the exceptional powers in managing enemies, the relatives of Joseph were guaranteed of plentiful endowments.

From above, they would have rich rain and dew. From underneath, the dirt would be provided with the fixings that would make sustenance and harvests. By uncommon perfect blessing, the richness among men and creatures would accommodate the unending productivity of the family.

26. To put it plainly, Joseph would dependably be viewed as a "sovereign among his siblings" (AV, isolate from his brethren). Hebrew nezeir designates "one set apart," or, "one who is isolated or sanctified for high obligations." The Nazarite was a man who had been given to God and by exceptional pledge was unalterably dedicated to him.

Ephraim, his child, was to have qualities that made for blessed commitment to satisfy God's motivation for one who was put energetically the standards so perfectly exemplified by Joseph. He was the sovereign among the tribes of Israel.

27. "Benjamin," the more youthful child of Rachel, was portrayed as a furious, hazardous wolf that could do extraordinary harm. The wolf is sharp and stealthy in his developments. During the evening he slips quietly among the sheep and grabs his prize.

Hebrew taraf intends to attack shreds. The early English word ravin signifies "to prey with greed." It discusses savage brutality. The night wolves could be as savage and ruinous in the early morning. Whenever they were prepared for the savage business of brutal conduct. Ehud, Saul, Jonathan were among the later relatives of Benjamin who gave proof of their warlike forces. The men of this tribe wound up noticeably well known for their bowmen and their slingers (cf. Jud. 5:14; 20:16).

Closing Days
(49:28-50:26)

28-33. At the point when Jacob had completed his address of gift, reproach, and revile, he conversed with his children of his moving toward death. In his last guidelines, he guided his children to take his body to Canaan for internment. "Cover me with my fathers in the give in," he stated, "that is in the savage of Ephron" (v. 29). He advised them that the family entombment put officially held the fiery debris of Abraham, Sarah, Isaac, Rebekah, and Leah.

Rachel was covered in a tomb close Bethelehem (cf. 35:19,20). When Jacob had completed his bearings "he got together his feet into the bed" and without a battle, "yielded up his soul (ruah) and go into the presenece of the individuals who had effectively gone into the other world (Sheol).

The Old Testament holy people were a long way from the New Testament origination of post-existence, yet even in that early day they knew about some bizarre observations as they remained within the sight of the expired individuals from the family. Sheol was the shadowy district where souls that had left the mortal body proceeded with their reality.

CHAPTER
FIFTY

Closing Days
(50:1-26)

Joseph uncovered his solid warmth for his dad in proceeded with enthusiastic show. Alternate children, likewise, most likely offered articulation to their adoration. To verify that Jacob's body was saved from disintegration for the long voyage to Hebron, Joseph approached his hirelings, the Egyptian physicans, to treat it, "and the doctors preserved Israel (v. 2).

The Egyptians were mindful so as to save the body of a perished individual with the goal that when the spirit came back to take up habitation once more, the body would be prepared for occupation. Egyptian mummies saved for quite a long time bear quiet observer to the amazing productivity of these embalmers. The word rapha' intends to "recuperate" or to "repair," by methods for surgery or prescriptions. Doctors were copious in Egypt, and it is conceivable that they directed the significant piece of the preserving.

At any rate, Jacob's body was embalmed for the excursion, and probably been very much safeguarded for the day of entombment. "The Egyptians grieved for him threescore and ten days" (v. 3). Maybe forty days were fundamental for the treating. Extra days were expected to finish the period off grieving, with the goal that seventy days at long last go before the excursion to Canaan started. The Egyptian country, keeping in mind Joseph, partook in the grieving.

4-6. In securing official consent to leave the kingdom, Joseph cited his dad's demand that he be covered in "my grave which I have digged." The Hebrew word Kara might be deciphered burrow or purchase. In Deut. 2:6 it appears to signify "buy," yet in this entry "digged" shows up the better interpretation.

Abraham purchased a plot of land from Ephron to be utilized as an entombment put for Sarah. There is no motivation to protest Jacob went into the buckle and "digged" from the stone his own particular grave.

7-13. With uncommon grandeur and show the Egyptian parade moved out from Goshen to make the long adventure to Hebron. Chariots and horsemen, alongside authorities of Pharaoh's court and every one of the children of Jacob, made up the burial service organization. The Egyptians "howled there with an exceptionally incredible and sore crying" (v. 10). The locals wondered about seeing the extensive organization of grievers; they had never observed anything like it. At the surrender of Machpelah "his sons....buried him." Israel had arrived at the finish of his exciting vocation.

14-21. Joseph, with his brothers, came back to Egypt to take up life once more. Quickly fear grabbed the more established children of Jacob. They figured Joseph may now turn upon them and correct full retribution for their wrongdoing of offering him into servitude. They "fell down before his face" (v. 18) in sadness, apology, and kindness. Joseph affectionately helped them that the hand to remember God had been in all that had happened, that the Lord had purposed it for good. He guaranteed them of his proceeded with adoration and guaranteed to accommodate their requirements amid the rest of the times of the starvation. Consistent with his sympathetic nature, "he addressed their hearts (v. 21; AV, spake kindly).

22-26. "So Joseph died....and he was placed in a coffin in Egypt." At the age of one hundred and ten Joseph passed on, having lived to be Jehovah's illustrative in a troublesome emergency in the life of His picked individuals. He claimed a grave vow from his siblings that they would guard his body until their arrival to Canaan, and after that convey it to his country for internment. Cf. Heb. 11:22: "By confidence Joseph, when his end was near, talked about the flight of the offspring of Israel: and gave charge concerning his bones."

His body was embalmed and put in a pine box ('aron) to anticipate the long excursion of forty years to Shechem. At the season of the Exodus, that mummy case was kept in the camp as an update that God's controlling hand is working out the awesome will in the greater part of life's battles (cf. Ex. 13:19).

Beginning closes with the reestablishment of the Lord's heavenly guarantees to his anointed ones and the test to move to the satisfaction of awesome purposes for Israel. Joseph had gone on. A Pharaoh "who new not Joseph" would happen upon the scene to change the upbeat connections gave by Joseph's knowledge, yet a Moses would ascend to take up the weight of administration. The interminable Lord would not overlook nor fall flat His kin. The rich purposes uncovered to the patriarchs would discover satisfaction in His own particular hour.

BIBLIOGRAPHY

Alleman, H. (1948) Old Testament Commentary. Philadelphia, PA.: Muhlenberg Press

Delitzch, F. (1899) A New Commentary On Genesis, (2 vols). Edinburgh, T&T Clark

Driver, S. R. (1948) The Book Of Genesis. Westminister Commentary. London, Eng.: Methuen

Eerdman, C.R. (1950) The Book Of Genesis. New York, NY.: Fleming H. Revell

Heertz, J. H. (1929) The Pentateuch And Haftorahs. London, Eng.: Oxford University Press

Pfeiffer, C. F. (1958) The Book Of Genesis. Grand Rapids, MI.: Baker Book House

Richardson, A. (1953) Genesis 1-11. Dondon, Eng.: Methuen

Ryle, H. E. (1914) The Book Of Genesis. Cambridge, New York, NY.: The University Press

The Holy Bible (1901) The American Standard Version. Nashville, TN.: Thomas Nelson & Sons (Used by Permission)

The Holy Bible (1964) The Authorized King James Version. Chicago, Ill.: J. G. Ferguson Company

The New Combined Bible Dictionary and Concordance (1968) Dallas, TX.: Baker Book Company

The Wycliff Bible Commentary (1968) Chicago, Ill.: The Moody Bible Institute Of Chicago

About The Author

The Reverend Dr. John Thomas Wylie is one who has dedicated his life to the work of God's Service, the service of others; and being a powerful witness for the Gospel of Our Lord and Savior Jesus Christ. Dr. Wylie was called into the Gospel Ministry June 1979, whereby in that same year he entered The American Baptist College of the American Baptist Theological Seminary, Nashville, Tennessee.

As a young Seminarian, he read every book available to him that would help him better his understanding of God as well as God's plan of Salvation and the Christian Faith. He made a commitment as a promising student that he would inspire others as God inspires him. He understood early in his ministry that we live in times where people question not only who God is; but whether miracles are real, whether or not man can make a change, and who the enemy is or if the enemy truly exists.

Dr. Wylie carried out his commitment to God, which has been one of excellence which led to his earning his Bachelors of Arts in Bible/

Theology/Pastoral Studies. Faithful and obedient to the call of God, he continued to matriculate in his studies earning his Masters of Ministry from Emmanuel Bible College, Nashville, Tennessee & Emmanuel Bible College, Rossville, Georgia. Still, inspired to please the Lord and do that which is well – pleasing in the Lord's sight, Dr. Wylie recently on March 2006, completed his Masters of Education degree with a concentration in Instructional Technology earned at The American Intercontinental University, Holloman Estates, Illinois. Dr. Wylie also previous to this, earned his Education Specialist Degree from Jones International University, Centennial, Colorado and his Doctorate of Theology from The Holy Trinity College and Seminary, St. Petersburg, Florida.

Dr. Wylie has served in the capacity of pastor at two congregations in Middle Tennessee and Southern Tennessee, as well as served as an Evangelistic Preacher, Teacher, Chaplain, Christian Educator, and finally a published author, writer of many great inspirational Christian Publications such as his first publication: ***"Only One God: Who Is He?" – published August 2002 via formally 1ˢᵗ books library (which is*** *now AuthorHouse Book Publishers located in Bloomington, Indiana & Milton Keynes, United Kingdom)* which caught the attention of **The Atlanta Journal Constitution Newspaper.**